Social Learning from Broadcast Television

Media Education Culture Technology

Robert Muffoletto, Series Editor

Computers in Education: Social, Political, and Historical Perspectives
Robert Muffoletto and Nancy Nelson Knupfer (eds.)

Social Learning from Broadcast Television
Karen Swan, Carla Meskill, and Steven DeMaio (eds.)

forthcoming

Technology and Education: Critical and Reflective Practices
Robert Muffoletto (ed.)

Social Learning from Broadcast Television

Edited by

Karen Swan
Carla Meskill
Steven DeMaio

University of Albany

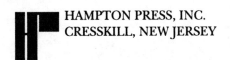

HAMPTON PRESS, INC.
CRESSKILL, NEW JERSEY

Printed in the United State of America

Library of Congress Cataloging-in-Publication Data

Social learning from broadcast television / edited by Karen Swan,
    Carla Meskill, Steven DeMaio.
        p. cm. – (Media education culture technology)
    Includes bibliographical references and indexes.
    ISBN 1-57273-096-X. – ISBN 1-57273-097-8
    1. Television and children. 2. Social learning. 3. Television-
-Social aspects. 4. Child development. I. Swan, Karen.
II. Meskill, Carla. III. DeMaio, Steven. IV. Series
HQ784.T4S63 1998
302.23'45'083–dc21   98-5190
                                                                    CIP

Hampton Press, Inc.
23 Broadway
Cresskill, NJ 07626

Contents

About the Contributors

John Black is a Professor in the Department of Communication, Computing, and Technology and in the Department of Developmental and Educational Psychology at Teachers College, Columbia University. He researches how people learn from text, video, computers, and multimedia. Prior to coming to Teachers College he was an Associate Professor of Psychology and Computer Science at Yale University. He has been a visiting research scientist at the IBM Thomas J. Watson Research Center.

Joseph Bowman is Assistant Professor of Instructional Technology, University at Albany, State University of New York, where he also directs the Center for Urban Youth and Technology. He holds a doctorate from Teachers Collect, Columbia University, where he taught computing, information management, and television products. Dr. Bowman has been involved in the development, design, and implementation of instructional technology in education for over 10 years.

David Buckingham is a lecturer in Media Education at the Institute of Education, London University, U.K. He has conducted several research studies on Children and television and on Media Education. His books include *Children Talking Television, Reading Audiences: Young People and the Media,* and *Moving Images: Children's Emotional Responses to Television.*

Robin Flanagan is a doctoral candidate in Educational Psychology at Teachers College, Columbia University working with John Black. SHe is doing research on the effect of media on children. Previously, she taught computer science at Duchess Community College, in Duchess County, NY.

Carla Meskill is a faculty member in the Department of Educational Theory and Practice, University at Albany, State University of New York. She also directs the Center for Electronic Language Learning and Research at the same institution. Her research includes investigation of the role of instructional technologies—especially multimedia technologies—in second language acquisition. Her work focuses on the interaction of media and language development.

Karen Swan holds a doctorate in Instructional Technology from Columbia University, and is an associate professor of the same in the School of Education in the State University of New York at Albany. Dr. Swan teaches courses on media and instruction, is director of the Learning Technologies Laboratory, and codirects the National Center for Research on Literature Teaching and Learning's Multimedia project. Her research is primarily in the area of the effects of media environments on learning, and she has published extensively in this area. Her most recent work includes journal articles on history and hypermedia, commercial multimedia literature applications, and social learning from television. She has also authored several multimedia and hypermedia applications, including the IBM Multimedia Sampler and Set On Freedom: The American Civil Rights Movement.

Rosemarie T. Truglio is an Assistant Professor of Communication and Education at Teachers College, Columbia University. She received her PhD in Developmental and Child Psychology from the University of Kansas. Through her research, she has investigated the effects of television on the cognitive and social development of children and adolescents. Specific content areas include children's early reading skills, viewer's reality judgments of televised content, gender roles, and how televised sexual portrayals contribute to adolescents' sexual socialization.

Introduction

Steven DeMaio

In recent years, the issue of social learning from broadcast television has been of interest to a wide range of researchers and observers. Social and behavioral literature with regard to television effects has been synthesized (Comstock with Paik, 1991), research has been conducted on children's cognitive perceptions of what they see on television (Simatos & Spencer, 1992), the particular nature of the exceptional child's learning from the medium has been explored (Sprafkin, Gadow, & Abelman, 1992), and even a cultural history of the impact of broadcast television on the American sociological and psychological landscape has been woven (Spigel, 1992). Clearly, the variety of different arenas in which the medium has been examined points to its perceived importance as a social force in modern society. Indeed, after reviewing over 2,500 studies on the effects of television on human behavior, in 1982 the National Institute of Mental Health concluded that not only was television a major socializing agent on American children, but that television viewing had nontrivial influences on how all people think and feel about the world around them, or what are sometimes called their *conceptions of social reality*. By recognizing the role of broadcast television in defining the social center of our culture and in establishing boundaries within which the public conceives the world around them, this report redefined a long-standing debate among television researchers as to whether the effects of television viewing on human behavior were powerful or minimal. Although the immediate effects of television viewing on behavior are minimal for most people, the report concluded, the long-term effects of television on people's conceptions of social reality are not.

People's conceptions of social reality involve not only what they view as acceptable and unacceptable behavior, what they value and what they believe others value, how they stereotype others, and what kind of a world, in general, they think they live in, but are also a kind of lens through which they view others, events in the world, and ultimately themselves—the glass, as it were, through which we see darkly. Television, too, is a lens through which we view the world. The average American spends 6 hours a day watching television. It is the major source of information for most Americans as well. It is important, therefore, to examine both the social reality being presented to use through broadcast television, and how we make meanings from that presentation.

As the role that television plays on the world stage expands, as the number of countries in which it has become a potent political, social, and economic force increases, and as the degree of its psychological and sociological power in countries where it has been important for decades grows, debates about its impact are becoming more frequent, more emotionally and politically charged, and more concerned with identifying what exactly gives the medium its supposed edge over other media with which it competes for space. Researchers, academics, politicians, and journalists, all themselves viewers of television, have attempted to articulate the essence of the medium. They talk about viewing patterns, formal features, violent content, social uses, educational drawbacks, educational benefits, family discourse settings, and a host of other categorizable aspects of television that are supposed to shed some light on the nature of the whole. No matter how "micro" the objects and/or subjects of analysis, the stated or implied goal is usually to essentialize some feature of the medium—that is, to reconcile some facts and/or conjectures and to arrive at some admittedly tentative point of resolution to be reopened later by the same or another observer. This is not to say that every examination of television attempts to articulate universalities about the medium or to put the matter to rest as it makes its concluding remarks; in fact, most do not. However, the suggestion of possible future resolution of previously discussed particularities is usually present. It might be said that there is an unconscious reductionist wish that underlies most examinations, although each particular study or discussion resists reductionism within the limits of what it explicitly argues. This is to say that most arguments about television take their particular angles on the medium or bring together several angles, and arrive at temporary ends, anticipating their being reopened later by examiners who will use them to arrive at new ends, and so on. Of course, this tendency can be said to characterize academic and rhetorical enterprise in general or, perhaps, to be inherent to such enterprise. Nonetheless, the question arises as to how to best safeguard against the reductionist wish while remaining conscious that no thoroughly effective method exists.

The editors of this book have decided that in order to emphasize the variety of dimensions of social learning from broadcast television and the breadth of research methodologies that can be used to study it, it is necessary not only to represent a host of different dimensions and methodologies in selecting chapters for inclusion, but also to resist the temptation to schematize and categorize what is treated in those chapters in order to arrive at a point of tentative resolution about the issue. Therefore, this text does not wish to unify its chapters in its introduction, but rather to dedicate most of the remaining space of that introduction to a brief discussion of the editors' views about representations of social reality that led to the choices about content and presentation that were made in putting this collection together.

Whether behind the camera in a high-tech studio, on the set of a prime-time sitcom, in front of the television in the family living room, or in the home of a nonnative speaker of English, conceptions and representations of social reality are constantly being negotiated. They cannot be identified, isolated, and then studied without reference to the contexts in which they are conceived or created and without awareness of the capacity to change and to influence each other. To conceive broadcast television, and the negotiated social learning that takes place in relation to it, as a totality (i.e., as a social arena that can be accounted for by a particular theoretical, psychological, or research model) is to deny the dynamic nature and complexity of the conceptions and representations of social reality that are constructed in interactions with the medium. An examination of broadcast television must be approached from a variety of angles (through many different lenses, if you will), in order to safeguard against reductionism. However, even a piece shot from many angles is in need of revision after time has passed and once angles never envisioned before have been conceived.

The chapters in *Social Learning from Broadcast Television* employ a variety of research methodologies and focus on a a variety of dimensions of the current broadcast television picture. Topics discussed range from content analyses of current programs, to an ethnographic study of how British children use television to gain power over parents and peers, to an examination of the historically contingent phenomena that surround the production and viewership of particular shows, to an analysis of the features of American sitcoms that play a role in the second language learning processes of nonnative speakers of English. The variety of angles from which social learning from broadcast television is examined in this text is not intended to suggest an "essence" or to totalize a phenomenon; rather, a wide range of vantage points from which to look at social learning is provided, so as to remain true to the notion that social realities, as portrayed on, created by, or constructed behind the scenes of television, are negotiable, ever-changing and mutually influencing constructs.

Therefore, the six chapters represented in this volume not only represent six different discussions about the issue of social learning from broadcast television, but also function as dialogues with the media scholar, communications media specialist, educational psychologist, classroom teacher, or interested viewer who reads them, and as dialogues with each other.

In chapter 1, Rosemarie Truglio addresses the issue of adolescent sexual socialization from television. From a content analysis conducted on a representative sample of 67 prime-time programs during 1991, Truglio identifies the lessons about sexual behavior and attitudes that are being taught. She then explores how these lessons are integrated into adolescents' sexual schemata, using interviews with 8th, 10th, and 12th graders to draw her conclusions. Among these conclusions is that the infiltration of unrealistic sexual messages into adolescents' real-world understanding of sexual behavior may lead to potentially dangerous consequences. On the other hand, Truglio argues, there is evidence that television may be used as a positive tool to disseminate important information to adolescents about sex.

An examination of the contextually bound, socially constructed nature of children's relationships with television is the focus of chapter 2. David Buckingham draws on his past research based on interviews with British children between the ages of 7 and 12. The research incorporates perspectives from cultural studies, but extends them by using analytical methods derived from discourse analysis and social semiotics. From this foundation, Buckingham has developed a social theory of children's use and understanding of television that challenges more traditional behaviorist and cognitivist perspectives. His particular emphases in this chapter are on how children define the effects of television in their discourse, how the context of viewing affects children's perceptions of sex and violence on television, and how children actively use notions of innocence and experience as a way of gaining power over each other and over adults.

In chapter 3, Robin Flanagan and John Black share the results of their study of the relationships between television viewing and learned helplessness and between watching an educational video and opting to work on difficult problems. Sixty-four third graders from three different classrooms at two schools served as subjects. Greater persistence was evidenced following nonmediated instruction. The authors propose two forms of learned helplessness in operation: logistical and automatic.

In chapter 4, Carla Meskill focuses on learners of English as a second language (ESL) in the United States. She examines the impact of the linguistic and cultural information that is transmitted via commercial television. The viewing habits of some two hundred ESL learners in U.S. public schools are examined in this chapter. Meskill argues that the particular features of the type of program which nonnative speakers of English prefer most—family situation comedies—are actually complementary to the goals of learning U.S. language and culture.

In chapter 5, Karen Swan looks at Saturday morning cartoons broadcast on U.S. television for a 21-month span between 1990 and 1992, after the Children's Television Act of 1990 went into effect. The block of time between 8:00 a.m. and 11:00 a.m. on Saturday mornings is the only block of programming on the three major U.S. television networks devoted exclusively to children. Swan examines the misrepresentative gender, ethnic, and age makeup of the societies portrayed in these cartoons and argues that their plots and themes are, on the whole, strikingly similar to those of the cartoons that accompanied the Saturday movie matinees of the past and to traditional fairy tales. However, she points out that current cartoons are bound up with a corporate ethic different from the individualism portrayed in earlier versions of the genre. Swan concludes with a look at the marketing of the programs and at Saturday morning commercials and commercialism, arguing that consumerism is central to both.

Chapter 6 presents the processes and outcomes of projects that involved urban minority children in all facets of television production. Joseph Bowman details the social and academic effects of empowering minority children through hands-on, minds-on contact with television in the making. Several years of disadvantaged youth behind word processors, editors, and video cameras reveal that these children-centered and production-centered activities build skills—both technical and academic—self-esteem, and a voice and sense of place in a world dominated by a medium that fails to represent who they are.

REFERENCES

Comstock, G. with Paik, H. (1991). *Television and the American child*. San Diego: Academic Press.

National Institute of Mental Health. (1982). *Television and behavior, Vol 1. Summary Report*. (DHHS Publication No. ADM 82-1195). Washington, DC: U.S. Government Printing Office.

Simatos, A., & Spencer, K. (1992). *Children and the media*. Liverpool: Manutius.

Spigel, L. (1992). *Make room for TV: Television and the family ideal in postwar America*. Chicago: University of Chicago Press.

Sprafkin, J., Gadow, K., & Abelman, R. (1992). *Television and the exceptional child: A forgotten audience*. Hillsdale, NJ: Erlbaum.

1

Television as a Sex Educator*

Rosemarie T. Truglio
Teachers College, Columbia University

During adolescence, interests in intimate interpersonal relationships and sexual feelings become intensified. According to Erickson (1968), adolescence is a period of development during which there is an increasing social need to find one's role in life as a sexual, productive, responsible adult with a reasonably consistent set of attitudes and values. Physiological changes coupled with perceptions of what is normative in one's peer group can lead to early initiation of sexual activity (Brooks-Gunn & Furstenberg, 1989).

Television, through its "realistic" portrayal of consistent and often explicit sexual messages, can be a powerful sex educator, particularly for viewers with limited experience and countervailing information (E.J. Roberts, 1982). With limited opportunities to observe intimate interpersonal behavior in real life, adolescents may often rely on mass-media models for sexual learning (Bandura & Walters, 1963). Television provides young people with an abundant source of information (both realistic and unrealistic) about intimate interpersonal relationships. Moreover, learning about romance and sexual behavior from television circumvents the embarrassment of direct questioning.

*The content analysis of 1991 prime time portrayals discussed in this chapter was supported by a Dean's Grant at Teachers College, Columbia University. The author expresses sincere appreciation to the graduate students involved in the development of the coding scheme and in the analyses of programs. Thanks to Christine Li, Jennifer Davis, Bruce Long, Dorothy McIntyre, Amy Patraka, and Sandy Wertheimer. This research was also aided by the generosity of the late John Condy and Cynthia Scheibe for providing access to their television archive. Special thanks to Ellen Meier for her helpful comments and suggestions throughout the development of this manuscript.

Public concern about adolescents' sexual socialization has been generated by the prevalence of sexual images in the media and by the incidence of teenage pregnancy and sexually transmitted diseases (STDs), especially AIDS. More than half of America's teenagers report having had sexual intercourse by age 17 (Louis Harris & Associates, 1986). Only one-third of these sexually active teens stated that they use contraceptives all the time. Although there is some evidence that condom use has increased during the 1980s (Forrest & Singh, 1990; Sonenstein, Pleck, & Ku, 1989), the majority of adolescents remain inconsistent users of condoms (Centers for Disease Control [CDC], 1992).

SOURCES OF SEXUAL INFORMATION

All states either mandate or recommend some type of sex education for students, and few provide balanced information on safer sex and abstinence (Britton, deMauro, & Gambrell, 1992). However, information adolescents most want involves the interpersonal aspects of sexuality (Gilbert & Bailis, 1980). Unfortunately comprehensive sex education courses providing in-depth discussion of the cognitive, affective, and skill components of sex are offered by only a minority of school districts (Kirby, 1984; Sonenstein & Pittman, 1984).

Parents often consider themselves resources for sexual information (E.J. Roberts, Kline, & Gagnon, 1978), and adolescents rated parents as their chief source of information about pregnancy and contraception (Louis Harris & Associates, 1986). Unfortunately, the scope and quality of parent-child discussions about sex is often limited, shallow, and infrequent. Noller and Bagi (1985) found that mothers and daughters were the only parent–child dyad in which any significant sex-related discussion occurred, but participants expressed low levels of self-disclosure and satisfaction. Correspondingly, among the two-thirds of all teenagers surveyed by Louis Harris & Associates (1986) who reported that they talked with their parents about how pregnancy is caused, only one-half of these teens discussed birth control.

As adolescents gradually discover their own particular sexual interests, they learn the sexual scripts provided to them by their social environment (Gagnon & Simon, 1973). These scripts include previous experiences, fantasies and expectations, stories from friends (Brooks-Gunn & Furstenburg, 1989), and media portrayals (E.J. Roberts, 1982). The task of integrating one's own sexuality (e.g., sexual feelings moral values) with these sexual scripts is the primary struggle of adolescent sexuality (Kimmel & Weiner, 1985). This process can be difficult because society conveys many contradictory messages about sex, and adolescents often do not have someone they can talk with regarding their sexual feelings and questions about sex.

In addition to parents, peers, and schools, children cite mass media (Darling & Hicks, 1982; Louis Harris & Associates, 1986), particularly television (Truglio, 1992), as a primary source of sexual information. Parents may want to be the ones to teach their children about sex, but realize they often compete with mass media's sexual curriculum (Louis Harris & Associates, 1987; E.J. Roberts et al., 1978). Television, which is in 98% of American households and turned on approximately 7 hours a day (Murray, 1993), has become a common source of socialization of American children. Considering the majority of children's viewing occurs during prime time (A. C. Nielsen, 1993) featuring programs designed for an adult audience, Greenberg et al. (1993b) estimated that young viewers are exposed to approximately 1,400 sexual acts per year, excluding daytime soap opera viewing.

The problem with turning to television for sexual information is that it is a *constructed reality* comprised of idealized and distorted images of sexual behavior. In the world of television, sex occurs more often between uncommitted than married couples; safer sexual practices are rarely considered; and potential negative consequences of intercourse occur infrequently (Greenberg et al., 1993b; Lowry & Towles, 1989a). Conversely, a survey of a nationally representative sample of 18- to 59-year-olds indicated that married people are more sexually active than their single counterparts (Laumann, Gagnon, Michael, & Michaels, 1994). Unprotected sexual practices among U.S. teenagers result in more than one million pregnancies each year, 85% of which are unintended (Alan Guttmacher Institute, 1994). Of the 3 million cases of sexually transmitted diseases (CDC, 1990), chlamydia is the most prevalent (CDC, 1989), but AIDS among 13- to 19-year-olds is rapidly increasing (CDC, 1994).[1]

With the premise that all television is educational (Palmer, Smith, & Strawser, 1993), the goal of this chapter is to discuss the sexual lessons taught by television in the 1990s. The basis of this discussion is a content analysis I conducted on 1991 prime-time broadcast programming. Although sexual portrayals extend well beyond prime-time television, broadcast television remains the source of most people's viewing (Dorr & Kunkel, 1990). Despite changes in media entertainment, with increased cable options, VCRs, satellite dishes, and video games, the prime-time share of broadcast television exceeds 80% (Comstock, 1993). The results of this study are discussed here in the context of how sexual portrayals have changed in response to the AIDS crisis, and the potential role television plays in adolescents' sexual socialization.

---

[1]As of June 30, 1995, 2,184 cases of AIDS among 13- to 19-year-olds were reported to the Centers for Disease Control. There were 17,745 cases of AIDS reported among 20- to 24-year-olds.

SEXUAL PORTRAYALS IN THE 1970s AND 1980s

Prior to the 1970s, the Broadcast Standards Departments of the major networks perpetuated and maintained a thoroughly puritanical TV world in which discussions about sex or physical intimacy were taboo. During the mid-1970s, however, viewers began to voice their concern about the number of sexual portrayals and the potential effects of sexual content portrayed on prime-time television programs (Franzblau, Sprafkin, & Rubinstein, 1977).

To assess the accuracy of public concerns, Franzblau et al. conducted the first content analysis of sexual portrayals on prime-time television programs in the 1975-1976 season. Surprisingly, the results of this investigation showed that less sensual forms of physical intimacy (e.g., nonaggressive touching) occurred more often than kissing, embracing, flirting and seductiveness, and sexual innuendoes. Furthermore, physically explicit sexual behaviors such as intercourse, rape, and homosexual behavior were never shown and verbal references to these behaviors were rare.

Over the years, however, sexual portrayals increased in frequency and explicitness (Greenberg et al., 1993a; Louis Harris & Associates, 1988; Lowry & Towles, 1989a; Silverman, Sprafkin, & Rubinstein, 1979;). The most dramatic increase in sexual content occurred during the 1978-1979 season (Sprafkin & Silverman, 1981). Kissing nearly doubled from an average of 4 acts to 7 acts per hour; acts of sexual innuendo occurred, on average, 13.6 times per hour. Of greater concern, verbal and implied references to sexual intercourse increased substantially from virtually none in 1975 to 1 reference per hour in 1978. During the late 1980s, physical, verbal, or implied references to sexual intercourse increased to approximately 2 acts per hour (Louis Harris & Associates, 1988; Lowry & Towles, 1989a).

In the television world, the range of sexual behaviors is unrealistically narrow, avoiding portrayals of controversial topics (e.g., contraception, abortion, and homosexuality); socially discouraged sexual behaviors (e.g., rape and incest); and modes of sexual gratifications (e.g., masturbation). Prostitution has been the most variable with increases and decreases over the years (Fernandez-Collado, Greenberg, Korzenny, & Atkin, 1978; Greenberg, Graef, Fernandez-Collado, Korzenny, & Atkin, 1980; Greenberg et al., 1993a) reaching its peak in 1978 with 1.38 references per hour (Silverman et al., 1979).

Extending beyond prime time, the most common sexual behaviors in daytime soaps are erotic touching and sexual intercourse (Greenberg, Abelman, & Neuendorf, 1981; Greenberg & D'Alessio, 1985; Lowry & Towles, 1989b). Although love in the afternoon is notorious for its sexual portrayals, sex on the soaps is mostly talked about, whereas prime-time sex has more visual scenes implying sexual intercourse and more suggestive sexual innuendoes about sex (Greenberg et al., 1993b). R-rated movies popular among adolescents have a higher proportion of visual portrayals than do broadcast television programs. Such viewing experiences contain on average 17.5 sexual acts per film; the most frequent is heterosexual sexual intercourse (Greenberg et al., 1993a).

Across all studies, it is the uncommitted individuals who are consistently more sexually active than married couples (Fernandez-Collado et al., 1978; Greenberg et al., 1980, 1993b; Travis, Phillips, & Williams, 1986). Moreover, despite the fact that safer sexual practices (e.g., contraceptive use) were not mentioned during the 1970s and rarely mentioned during the 1980s (Louis Harris & Associates, 1988; Lowry & Towles, 1989a), potential negative consequences of unprotected sexual activity occurred infrequently (Lowry & Towles 1989a; Travis et al., 1986). Any discussion of pregnancy and STD prevention was more likely to occur on prime time, whereas it was nonexistent on daytime soaps (Lowry & Towles, 1989b).

In response to the AIDS epidemic and teenage pregnancy, television's responsibility to portray the consequences of sex as well as the pleasures finally began to receive some attention (Hill, 1987). In recent years, advocacy groups have had some success in getting safer sexual practices into programming (Montgomery, 1990). One major breakthrough has been the freedom to mention the word *condom* (although rarely acted on) instead of referring to it as a thingamabob or love glove (Wakefield, 1987). Messages about pregnancy and STD prevention, however, remain minuscule in relation to the frequency of sexual intercourse (Louis Harris & Associates, 1988; Lowry & Towles, 1989a).

A CONTENT ANALYSIS OF 1991 PRIME-TIME PROGRAMMING

A representative sample of 109 prime-time programs, excluding movies, were recorded across the four commercial networks; namely, ABC, CBS, NBC, and FOX. Prime-time was defined as 8 to 11 p.m. (Eastern time) Monday through Saturday and 7 to 11 p.m. on Sunday. The sample consisted of 69.5 hours of programming (including commercials, which were not analyzed).

The majority of programs (n = 67) appeared on ABC, CBS, and NBC during the months of March, June, September, and December of 1991. This sample of programs was collected by The Center for Research on the Effects of Television at Cornell University and Ithaca College. For each month, a composite week was composed of a randomly selected day of the week. On each day channels across the three networks were changed every hour using a randomized block design. An independent sampling of

FOX consisted of 42 programs airing during the months of July, September, and November of 1991. To date, this study is the most comprehensive investigation of sexual behavior, its consequences, and attitudes expressed about sexual intercourse across the four commercial networks.

Four trained coders documented the frequency of physical, verbal and implied instances of couples' nonsexual behavior (kissing, hugging, and touching) and sexual behavior (kissing, hugging, touching, suggestiveness/innuendo, and heterosexual intercourse). Heterosexual intercourse was classified as any direct physical, verbal, or contextually implied reference. Indirect or implied verbal references were coded as innuendo. Interrater reliability across sexual and nonsexual behavior was .75. The distinction between nonsexual and sexual behavior is that the intent of sexual behavior is to arouse another sexually.

To assess changes in the network's portrayal of safer sexual practices, all references to contraception, particularly condoms, pregnancy, and sexually transmitted diseases were coded. Other sexual behaviors coded were: (a) homosexuality; (b) socially discouraged practices (incest, pederosis, prostitution, and aggressive sexual acts); and (c) socially discouraged modes of sexual gratifications (exhibitionism, fetishism, masturbation, pornography and striptease, transvestism and transsexualism, voyeurism, and other unique sexual behavior). Interrater reliability for safer sexual practices was .80; for socially discouraged sexual behavior and modes of sexual gratification, interrater reliability was .85.

The basic coding procedures and operational definitions for the aforementioned categories were adapted from Silverman, Sprafkin, and Rubinstein (1978); however, several modifications were made. First, a distinction was made between those couples engaged in the sexual behavior (participants) and observers of the behavior (nonparticipants' comments). In addition, the relationship between the individuals engaged in the behavior was coded as: married, committed, married but not to each other, and uncommitted. A committed relationship was defined as a couple who are engaged to each other, are living together, or are exclusively dating each other. Other modifications included: (a) the age of characters (teen or adult); and (b) attitudes about heterosexual intercourse expressed by both participants and nonparticipants. Interrater reliability for age, relationships, and attitudes about intercourse were .99, .95, and .79, respectively.

Television's Sexual Lessons for the 1990s

Sex on prime-time television has become more pervasive in 1990s, but it remains largely in the form of suggestiveness/innuendo and direct verbal references to sexual intercourse. Interpersonal behaviors between couples, the majority of whom were adults (80.6%), were more likely to be sexually arousing than nonsexual (28.2 versus 20.6, respectively). Since 1988, sexual portrayals, excluding touching, increased by 4.6 sexual acts per hour. This comparison is based on the results reported by Louis Harris and Associates (1988), who used a similar coding scheme but did not include touching. The behaviors with the greatest increase were sexual suggestiveness and innuendo, which doubled from 8.9 acts to 16.7 acts per hour, and direct references to heterosexual intercourse, which increased by 1.5 acts for a total of 3.4 acts per hour.

Surprisingly, there was not a significant difference in the overall amount of sexual behavior shown on the FOX compared to the three other networks (See Table 1.1 for frequencies). Fox, however, did have a slightly higher number of references to sexual intercourse. FOX has a reputation for testing the limits of what can be shown on prime-time television with programs such as *Beverly Hills 90210*, *In Living Color*, *Married With Children*, and *True Colors*. In fact, the only portrayal of physical intercourse (i.e., a man and woman clearly engaged in the act of intercourse partially covered by a blanket) appeared on *In Living Color*.

Consistent with previous findings, unmarried couples were more sexually active than their committed or married counterparts (See Table 1.2 for frequencies). Furthermore, the integration of safer sexual practices in any form has remained remarkably low. The mention of any form of pregnancy or STD prevention equaled only 16 references for the entire sample.

Even though uncommitted couples engage in unprotected sexual intercourse, pregnancies are few and the transmission of STDs is virtually nonexistent. Married couples, on the other hand, are less likely to engage in sex, but are more likely to get pregnant than their single counterparts (1.9 references versus .51 for married couples). There were no references to abortion.

Although sex among uncommitted couples appears to associated with few physical consequences, it is not always portrayed as positive. Among unmarried couples, only 43.5% expressed a positive attitude about their coital experience. Nonparticipants who frequently voiced their opinions about sexual intercourse (as indicated in Table 1.2) tended to be critical of intercourse among uncommitted partners. Only 18% of nonparticipants expressed a positive attitude about unmarried intercourse and 24.5% had a negative reaction. This pattern is consistent with the results reported by Greenberg et al. (1993b; see Table 1.3 for comparisons).

As in the real world, attitudes about sex on television are not always clearly stated. A sizable number of neutral statements about sex among uncommitted individuals were mentioned by both participants and nonparticipants (18.3% and 39.6%, respectively). Correspondingly, all television is not monolithic; consequently, attitudes about sex vary

Table 1.1. Nonsexual and Sexual Behaviors Per Hour of Programming.

	ABC, CBS, NBC		FOX	
	Physical	Verbal	Physical	Verbal
Nonsexual Behaviors:				
Kiss				
Participant	1.40	.19	.96	.07
Nonparticipant	-	.04		.07
Hug				
Participant	2.45	.06	1.57	.01
Nonparticipant	-	.01	-	.01
Touch				
Participant	9.08	.03	4.68	-
Nonparticipant	-	-	-	-
Total	13.23		7.38	
	(20.6 acts per hour)			

	ABC, CBS, NBC			FOX		
	Physical	Verbal	Implied	Physical	Verbal	Implied
Sexual Behaviors:						
Kiss						
Participant	1.80	.20	.01	1.45	.30	-
Nonparticipant	-	.07	-	-	.09	-
(Subtotal)	**(2.08)**			**(1.84)**		
Hug						
Participant	.92	.01	-	.79	.03	-
Nonparticipant	-	.03	-	-	-	-
(Subtotal)	**(.96)**			**(.82)**		
Touch						
Participant	1.09	.07	.01	1.03	.13	.01
Nonparticipant	-	.01	-	-	.10	-
(Subtotal)	**(1.18)**			**(1.27)**		
Suggestiveness/ Sexual Innuendo						
Participant	2.23	4.43	-	2.00	4.17	-
Nonparticipant	-	2.00	-	-	1.84	-
(Subtotal)	**(8.66)**			**(8.01)**		
Intercourse						
Participant	-	.62	.17	.03	.79	.27
Nonparticipant	-	.73	-	-	.79	-
(Subtotal)	**(1.52)**			**(1.88)**		
Total, all sexual acts	14.4			13.8		
	(28.2 acts per hour)					

Table 1.2. Sexual Activity Collapsed Across Networks by Type of Relationship.

	Physical	Verbal	Implied	Total
Kiss				
Married/Committed	.63	.04	.01	.68
Unmarried	2.63	.59	-	3.22
Unknown	-	.03	-	.03
Hug				
Married/Committed	.20	-	-	.20
Unmarried	1.51	.07	-	1.58
Unknown	-	-	-	-
Touch				
Married/Committed	.28	.04	-	.32
Unmarried	1.84	.24	.03	2.11
Unknown	-	.03	-	.03
Suggestiveness/ Innuendo				
Married/Committed	.24	1.47	-	1.71
Unmarried	3.99	10.49	-	14.48
Unknown	-	.48	-	.48
Intercourse				
Married/Committed	-	.36	.09	.45
Unmarried	.03	2.33	.36	2.72
Unknown	-	.24	-	.24
Total	(11.35)	(16.41)	(.49)	(28.25)

across programs. Consistent with its racy reputation, the characters on FOX programming expressed the most favorable attitudes about uncommitted sexual relations, whereas the other commercial networks were more conservative in their discussion of sexual intercourse.

In proportion to the overall amount of sexual content on television, references to homosexuality and socially discouraged sexual practices and gratification remain remarkably low. Physical portrayals of homosexuality remain scarce. Moreover, the majority of the verbal references occur in a comical context and are frequently derogatory. Of the socially discouraged behaviors, sexually explicit materials (e.g., pornographic magazines and films) and striptease were most common. Not surprisingly, FOX programming, compared to the other networks, was most liberal in their integration of voyeurism, transsexual/transvestism, prostitution, rape, fetishism, and incest. None of the networks dealt with masturbation, exhibitionism, and pederosis.

Table 1.3. Percentage of Participants' and Nonparticipants' Attitudes About Intercourse by Relationship Comparing FOX to the Other Networks.

	ABC, CBS, NBC						FOX					
	Married/ Committed		Not Committed		Unknown		Married/ Committed		Not Committed		Unknown	
	%	(f)	%	(f)	%	(f)	%	(f)	%	(f)	%	(f)
Participants:												
Positive	5.3	(7)	12.2	(16)	-		3.0	(4)	31.3	(41)	.76	(1)
Negative	3.8	(5)	11.4	(15)	-		3.8	(5)	4.6	(6)	-	
Neutral	.8	(1)	6.9	(9)	1.5	(2)	3.0	(4)	11.4	(15)	-	
Nonparticipants:												
Positive	.9	(1)	1.9	(2)	-		-		16.0	(17)	4.7	(5)
Negative	.9	(1)	13.2	(14)	5.7	(6)	2.8	(3)	11.3	(12)	-	
Neutral	-		24.5	(26)	.9	(1)	-		15.1	(16)	1.9	(2)

CONCLUSION/IMPLICATIONS

In spite of the appeals by educators, researchers, and parents, television continues to provide viewers with a distorted and unrealistic depiction of intimate interpersonal relationships. In the TV world, drama and passion prevail over the integration of crucial factual information about safer sexual practices. Sexual behaviors have steadily increased over the years and unmarried couples are portrayed as the most sexually active. Perhaps the most disturbing finding is that risk is still largely unassociated with unprotected sexual intercourse.

Prime-time programming continues to resist the discussion of and/or portrayal of controversial issues such as pregnancy or STD prevention, AIDS, and homosexuality. Condoms are almost never referred to or used; concern about STDs is virtually nonexistent; and sexual behavior among homosexual couples is strictly taboo. The only consequence of unprotected sex appears to be pregnancy, but the majority of pregnancies occurred as a result of married intercourse—the couples who are the least likely to have sex on television.

A single content analyses cannot capture all sexual behavior, particularly examples of responsible programming. In fairness to the indus-

Table 1.4. Socially Discouraged Sexual Behavior and Modes of Gratification.

	ABC, CBS, NBC			FOX		
	Physical	Verbal	Implied	Physical	Verbal	Implied
Pornography/ Striptease	1.00	.59	.04	.65	.59	-
(Total)		(1.63)			(1.24)	
Voyeurism	.14	.22	-	.32	.26 -	
(Total)		(.36)			(.58)	
Transsexual/ Transvestism	.03	.13	-	.10	.42	-
(Total)		(.16)			(.52)	
Prostitution	.03	.17	-	.06	.10	-
(Total)		(.20)			(.16)	
Aggressive Sexual Acts	.03	.01	-	.10	.16	-
(Total)		(.04)			(.26)	
Fetishism	-	-	-	.06	.04	.01
(Total)					(.11)	
Incest	-	-	.01	-	.07	-
Masturbation	-	-	-	-	-	-
Pederosis	-	-	-	-	-	-
Exhibitionism	-	-	-	-	-	-
Other[a]	.03	.42	-	.04	.16 -	
(Total)		(.45)			(.20)	

[a]Other was defined as any socially discouraged sexual behavior not belonging to any of the defined categories (e.g., bestiality).

try, there are examples of informative and responsible portrayals of sex. Programs have begun to integrate explicit and implicit references to condom use and ABC's Afterschool Specials have tackled issues such as unwanted teen pregnancy ("Jacqui's Dilemma") and AIDS as a result of unprotected teen sex ("A Question of Sex").

The problem, however, is that such responsible portrayals are far and few between. Montgomery (1990), for instance, found that although the commercial networks took great care to ensure that programs depicting AIDS provided viewers with a fair and accurate portrayal of the disease, the cumulative message about how AIDS is contracted was highly distorted. In the world of entertainment television, the overwhelming majority of people with AIDS were women and children, and the most common means of transmission was through blood transfusions.

Content analyses provide an overall picture of television's "sexual lessons," but inferences cannot be made from these data about possible effects on viewers. Theoretical frameworks such as social learning theory (Bandura, 1986), schema theory (Fiske & Taylor, 1991) and cultivation (Gerbner, Gross, Morgan, & Signorielli, 1980), support the view that television can have an effect on adolescents' sexual socialization. To determine the exact effects and the conditions under which adolescents process and incorporate televised sexual portrayals into their sexual attitudes, beliefs, and behavior, systematic experimental and longitudinal research must be conducted.

According to social learning theory, positive messages received from experiencing sexual behavior vicariously through the sexual prowess of television characters may encourage viewer's sexual activity. The decision to engage in sexual behavior, however, also depends on one's moral standards, perceived ability to express one's sexual feelings, and perceived consequences of prospective actions. As indicated by content analyses, sexual intercourse on television is not always portrayed in a positive manner. There are disappointments, regrets, and criticisms from others.

The principles of schema theory suggest that adolescents' schemata for sexual behavior can be formed by frequent exposure to sexual content on television. Because many of these portrayals provide similar messages and countervailing information is limited, sexual schemata may be strengthened rather than modified. Correspondingly, cultivation theory suggests that adolescents' sexual attitudes and beliefs will be mainstreamed by the consistent and repetitive "sexual lessons" shown across television programs.

Due to the controversial nature of this research only a few studies have investigated the effects of televised sexual portrayals on adolescents' sexual experiences. Baran (1976a, 1976b) found that adolescents and college students who perceived television characters as sexually competent and as enjoying their sexual experiences were less satisfied with their own first coital experience. Moreover, the perceived sexual pleasure of television characters was associated with college students' subsequent sexual dissatisfaction (Baran, 1976b). Brown & Newcomer (1991) found that the proportion of adolescents' "sexy" viewing was positively related to sexual activity. The total amount of viewing and the frequency of sexy viewing, however, were not significantly associated with adolescents' sexual experience. Peterson, Moore, and Furstenberg (1991) also found a relation between television viewing and sexual activity, but its association was true only for adolescent males.

Although the research on the effects of televised sexual portrayals on adolescents sexual socialization is limited and the correlational links weak, it is naive to dismiss television's role in the sexual education of youth. As D.F. Roberts (1993) posited, it is unproductive to search for massive media effects or equate massive with importance. Rather, it is imperative that we have a clearer understanding of the conditions under which adolescents most vulnerable to integrating fictional information about sexual behavior into their real-life sexual schemata. The consequences of such learning can lead to risky behavior and ultimately potentially negative consequences.

Although most adolescents are skeptics when judging the realism of sexual portrayals on television, sizable minorities believe that television provides a realistic picture of sexually transmitted diseases (45%), pregnancy and the consequences of sex (41%), and people making love (21%; Louis Harris & Associates, 1987). On average, adolescents know that television is a "window" into a world, but not necessarily into the real world. Truglio (1990) found that adolescents do differentiate between sexual events portrayed in fictional television programs from those occurring in real life. A distinct separation between real life and televised sexual behavior, however, may not be true for all adolescent viewers.

The socializing effects of sexual content may be moderated or mediated by viewer characteristics such as limited sexual knowledge and experience, the perceived social realism of portrayals, and the personal relevance of sexual scripts. For instance, adolescents who used television as a source for sexual information and perceived television's portrayals as realistic were more likely to incorporate television's sexual messages into their real-life sexual schemata than were adolescents more skeptical of television's portrayals of interpersonal relationships (Truglio, 1990). For some adolescent viewers, television provides an opportunity to learn more about sex, love, and romance, but for others the content may be judged as irrelevant or are less enamored with romantic fantasy (Brown, White, & Nikopoulou, 1993). Furthermore, the credibility and realism of sexual portrayals are lessened when compared to young adults' real-life sexual experiences (Courtright & Baran, 1980).

Parents can also be influential in reducing the potential socializing effects of television's sexual lessons by providing their children adequate countervailing information. Peterson et al. (1991) found that adolescent males who watched television with their parents were less likely to be sexually active. In contrast, viewing apart from parents was positively related to boy's sexual experience. These results may be indicative of parents seizing the opportunity to discuss the underlying messages of sexual portrayals. Television can be a useful springboard for parents to express their values and expectations and to disapprove of behavior deemed inappropriate.

Television can be a powerful sex educator, but the lessons remain unrealistic and potentially dangerous if adolescents integrate TV scenarios into their sexual schemata. Future content analyses need to use consistent definitions to track "sexual lessons" on television. Furthermore, a commitment must be made to investigate how adolescents interpret mass media's sexual portrayals.

Parents, teachers, and the media industry all need to take some responsibility in the sexual education of youth. In the interest of our youth, a compromise needs to be reached between the industry's right to artistic freedom and societal desires to protect youth from potentially negative consequences of unprotected sex (Roberts, 1993). Potential socializing effects of sexual content can be effectively diminished through open and frank discussions about the facts and intricacies of intimate interpersonal relationships. Instead of being embarrassed or intimated by factual or fictional sexual portrayals on television, parents should discuss program content and exert their role as the primary sex educator.

REFERENCES

A. C. Nielsen Company. (1993). *Nielsen media research: 1992-1993 report on television*. Northbrook, IL: Author.

Alan Guttmacher Institute. (1994). *Facts in brief. Abortion in the United States*. Washington, DC: Author.

Bandura, A. (1986). *Social foundations of thought and action. A social cognitive theory*. Englewood Cliffs, NJ: Prentice-Hall.

Bandura, A., & Walters, H. (1963). *Social learning and personality development*. New York: Holt, Rinehart & Winston.

Baran, S. J. (1976a). Sex on TV and adolescent sexual self-image. *Journal of Broadcasting, 20*(1), 61-68.

Baran, S. J. (1976b). How TV and film portrayals affect sexual satisfaction in college students. *Journalism Quarterly, 53*, 468-473.

Britton, P. O., deMauro, D., & Gambrell, A. E. (1992, November). HIV/AIDS education for schools finds states make progress but work remains. *SEICUS Report, 21*(1), 1-8.

Brooks-Gunn, J., & Furstenberg, F. F. (1989). Adolescent sexual behavior. *American Psychologist, 44*, 249-257.

Brown, J. D., & Newcomer, S. F. (1991). Television viewing and adolescents' sexual behavior. *Journal of Homosexuality, 21*(1/2), 77-91.

Brown, J. D., White, A. B., & Nikopoulou, L. (1993). Disinterest, intrigue, resistance: Early adolescent girls' use of sexual media content. In B. S. Greenberg, J. D. Brown, & N. L. Buerkel-Rothfuss (Eds.), *Media, sex and the adolescent* (pp. 177-195). Cresskill, NJ: Hampton Press.

Centers for Disease Control. (1989). *Division of STD/HIV Prevention, Annual report.* Atlanta, GA: Author.

Centers for Disease Control. (1990). *Division of STD/HIV Prevention, Annual report.* Atlanta, GA: Author.

Centers for Disease Control. (1992, October). *HIV/AIDS prevention newsletter.* Atlanta, GA: Author.

Centers for Disease Control. (1994, October). *CDC FAX information service, CDC semi-annual HIV/AIDS survelliance report.* Atlanta, GA: Author.

Comstock, G. (1993). The medium and the society: The role of television in American life. In G. L. Berry & J. Keiko Asamen (Eds.), *Children and television. Images in a changing sociocultural world* (pp. 117-131). Newbury Park, CA: Sage

Courtright, J. A., & Baran, S. J. (1980). The acquisition of sexual information by young people. *Journalism Quarterly, 57*(1), 107-114.

Darling, C. A., & Hicks, M. W. (1982). Parental influence on adolescent sexuality: Implications for parents as educators. *Journal of Youth and Adolescents, 11*, 231-245.

Dorr, A., & Kunkel, D. (1990). Children and the media environment. Change and constancy amid change. *Communication Research, 17*(1), 5-25.

Erickson, E. (1968). *Identity: Youth and crisis.* New York: Norton.

Fernandez-Collado, C. F., Greenberg, B. S., Korzenny, F., & Atkin, C. K. (1978). Sexual intimacy and drug use in TV series. *Journal of Communication, 28*(3), 30-37.

Fiske, S. T., & Taylor, S. E. (1991). *Social cognition* (2nd ed.). New York: McGraw-Hill.

Forrest, J. D., & Singh, S. (1990). The sexual and reproductive behavior of American women, 1982-1988. *Family Planning Perspectives, 22*, 206-214.

Franzblau, S., Sprafkin, J. N., & Rubinstein, E. A. (1977). Sex on TV: A content analysis. *Journal of Communication, 27*(2), 164-170.

Gagnon, J. J., & Simon, W. (1973). *Sexual conduct: The social sources of human sexuality.* Chicago: Aldine.

Gerbner, G., Gross, L., Morgan, M., & Signorielli, N. (1980). The "mainstreaming" of America: Violence profile No. 11. *Journal of Communication, 30*(3), 19-29.

Gilbert, F. S., & Bailis, K. L. (1980). Sex education in the home: An empirical task analysis. *The Journal of Sex Research, 16*(2), 148-161.

Greenberg, B. S., Abelman, R., & Neuendorf, K. (1981). Sex on the soap operas: Afternoon delight. *Journal of Communication, 31*(3), 83-89.

Greenberg, B. S., & D'Alessio, D. (1985). Quantity and quality of sex in the soaps. *Journal of Broadcasting and Electronic Media, 29*(3), 309-321.

Greenberg, B. S., Graef, D., Fernandez-Collado, C., Korzenny, F., & Atkin, C. K. (1980). Sexual intimacy on commercial TV during prime time. *Journalism Quarterly, 57*(2), 211-215.

Greenberg, B. S., Siemicki, M., Dorfman, S., Heeter, C., Stanley, C., Soderman, A., & Linsangan, R. (1993a). Sex content in R-rated films viewed by adolescents. In B. S. Greenberg, J. D. Brown, & N. L. Buerkel-Rothfuss (Eds.), *Media, sex and the adolescent* (pp. 45-58). Cresskill, NJ: Hampton Press.

Greenberg, B. S., Stanley, C., Siemicki, M., Heeter, C., Soderman, A., & Linsangan, R. (1993b). Sex content on soaps and prime-time television series most viewed by adolescents. In B. S. Greenberg, J. D. Brown, & N. L. Buerkel-Rothfuss (Eds.), *Media, sex and the adolescent* (pp. 29-44). Cresskill, NJ: Hampton Press.

Hill, D. (1987, August 8). Is TV sex getting bolder? *TV Guide*, pp. 2-5.

Kimmel, D. C., & Weiner, I. (1985). *Adolescence: A developmental transition.* Hillsdale, NJ: Erlbaum.

Kirby, D. (1984). *Sexuality education: An evaluation of programs and their effects. An executive summary.* Santa Cruz, CA: Network Publications.

Laumann, E. O., Gagnon, J. H., Michael, R. T., & Michaels, S. (1994). *The social organization of sexuality. Sexual practices in the United States.* Chicago: The University of Chicago Press.

Louis Harris & Associates, Inc. (1986). *American teens speak: Sex, myths, TV, and birth control.* New York: Planned Parenthood Federation of America.

Louis Harris & Associates, Inc. (1987). *Attitudes about television, sex, and contraceptive advertising.* New York: Author.

Louis Harris & Associates, Inc. (1988). *Sexual material on American network television during the 1987-1988 season.* New York: Planned Parenthood Federation of America.

Lowry, D. T., & Towles, D. E. (1989a). Prime time TV portrayals of sex, contraception and venereal diseases. *Journalism Quarterly, 66*(2), 327-352.

Lowry, D. T., & Towles, D. E. (1989b). Soap operas' portrayals of sex, contraception, and sexually transmitted diseases. *Journal of Communication, 39*(2), 76-83.

Montgomery, K. C. (1990). Promoting health through entertainment television. In C. Atkin & L. Wallack (Eds.), *Mass communication and public health. Complexities and conflicts* (pp. 114-128). Newbury Park, CA: Sage .

Murray, J. P. (1993). The developing child in a multimedia society. In G. L. Berry, & J. Keiko Asamen (Eds.), *Children and television. Images in a changing sociocultural world* (pp. 9-22). Newbury Park, CA: Sage.

Noller, P., & Bagi, S. (1985). Parent-adolescent communication. *Journal of Adolescence, 8*, 125-144.

Palmer, E. L., Smith, K. T., & Strawser, K. S. (1993). Rubik's Tube: Developing a child's television world view. In G. L. Berry & J. Keiko Asamen (Eds.), *Children and television. Images in a changing sociocultural world* (pp. 143-154). Newbury Park, CA: Sage.

Peterson, J. L., Moore, K. A., & Furstenberg, F. F. (1991). Television viewing and early initiation of sexual intercourse: Is there a link? *Journal of Homosexuality, 21*(1/2), 92-118.

Roberts, D. F. (1993). Adolescents and the mass media: From "Leave it to Beaver" to "Beverly Hills 90210." *Teachers College Record, 94*(3), 629-644.

Roberts, E. J. (1982). Television and sexual learning in childhood. In D. Pearl, L. Bouthilet, & J. Lazar (Eds.), *Television and behavior: Ten years of scientific progress and implications for the eighties Vol. 2* (pp. 209-223). Washington, DC: National Institute of Mental Health.

Roberts, E. J., Kline, D., & Gagnon, J. (1978). *Family life and sexual learning: A study of the role of parents in the sexual learning of children.* Cambridge, MA: Population Education Inc.

Silverman, L. T., Sprafkin, J. N., & Rubinstein, E. A. (1978). *Sex on television. A content analysis of the 1977-1988 prime-time programs.* Stony Brook, NY: Brookdale International Institute.

Silverman, L. T., Sprafkin, J. N., & Rubinstein, E. A. (1979). Physical contact and sexual behavior on prime-time TV. *Journal of Communication, 29*(1), 33-43.

Sonenstein, F. L., & Pittman, K. J. (1984). The availability of sex education in large city school districts. *Family Planning Perspectives, 16*(1), 19-25.

Sonenstein, F. L., Pleck, J. H., & Ku, L. C. (1989). Sexual activity, condom use and AIDS awareness among adolescent males. *Family Planning Perspectives, 21,* 152-158.

Sprafkin, J. N., & Silverman, L. T. (1981). Update: Physically intimate and sexual behavior on prime-time television, 1978-79. *Journal of Communication, 31*(1), 34-40.

Travis, L., Phillips, S., & Williams, T. M. (1986, June). *Television portrayals of sex and romance: What might children be learning?* Poster presented at the annual meeting of the Canadian Psychological Association, Toronto, Canada.

Truglio, R. T. (1990). *The role of prime-time television viewing in the sexual socialization of adolescents.* Unpublished doctoral dissertation, University of Kansas, Lawrence, KS.

Truglio, R. T. (1992, March). Adolescents' use of prime-time television for sexual information: What are the risks? In M. Danilo (Chair), *Health behavior and risk-taking during adolescents.* Symposium conducted at the Society for Research on Adolescents, Washington, D.C.

Wakefield, D. (1987, November 7). Teen sex and TV: How the medium has grown up. *TV Guide,* pp. 4-5.

2

Doing Them Harm?
Children's Conceptions of the
Negative Effects of Television

David Buckingham
University of London

Public debates about children and television have been almost exclusively dominated by arguments about the negative effects of the medium. As this chapter was written, the British press was full of reports about the murder of a 2-year-old child, Jamie Bulger, and the possibility that his young killers might have been led to commit the crime as a result of viewing violent videotapes. The lack of evidence in this case has not prevented an out-pouring of moral condemnation, in which familiar arguments about the irresistible power of moving images have been reasserted yet again in all their stark simplicity. Meanwhile, in justifying the chaotic changes in gov-ernment policy on education, ministers have mounted a series of attacks on the influence of television, and on the teaching of popular culture in schools. High-profile speeches have repeatedly condemned the "mindless voyeurism" of popular soap operas and the "sloppy speech" and immorali-ty they apparently promote, in favor of a renewed emphasis on the tradi-tional values of the literary classics. However, these are only the most recent examples of what has become an almost obsessive preoccupation among politicians and social commentators. Television has come to be seen as a primary cause—indeed an embodiment—of social and cultural disorder. It is routinely blamed, not merely for violence and delinquency, but also for the decline of the family and of organized religion, and for the propagation of racism, sexism, militarism, consumerism, and just about any other objectionable ideology one might care to name.

Such arguments about the negative effects of new media have in fact recurred throughout history (Buckingham, 1993a; Lusted, 1985; Pearson, 1984). One can find many echoes of these contemporary con-cerns in the campaigns against so called "horror comics" in the 1950s, and the anxieties about film and juvenile delinquency in the late 1920s. Indeed, it is possible to trace such concerns through the debates about popular drama and literature in the 18th and 19th centuries, back as far as the ancient Greek philosopher Plato, who proposed to ban the dramatic poets from his ideal republic on the grounds of their negative influence on impressionable young minds.

Such arguments also have an appeal right across the political spectrum. Although concerns about immorality and violence have been traditionally (although by no means exclusively) dominated by the political right, they have a great deal in common with the criticisms of stereotyping and "consumerism" made by many on the left. Both perspectives tend to regard television as extraordinarily powerful, and children as effectively powerless. Children are seen here as vulnerable and impressionable, mere passive victims whose minds are irresistibly molded by the negative messages that are seen to bombard and manipulate them.

As numerous critics have argued, these debates often serve to displace attention from more complex underlying causes, which we may actively wish to avoid acknowledging (Connell, 1984). For example, to blame television for the decline of the family—if indeed it can be seen to be in decline—is clearly to ignore the more complex reasons why that institution may be changing, and indeed may *need* to change. Likewise, to blame television for the perpetuation of racism or sexism is to ignore the much more complex and deep-seated structural reasons for these phenomena—and indeed to neglect the highly ambiguous role that television plays within them. The problem here is not merely that the positive effects of television—its contribution to children's learning about the world, and indeed the diverse pleasures that it offers them—are almost entirely ignored. It is also that the influence of the medium is so massively overstated, and the critical abilities of children so poorly acknowledged. However, such arguments do not merely oversimplify the nature of children's relationship with television: they also represent a way of avoiding genuine social problems. In using television as a convenient scapegoat for what is wrong with the world, we are almost invariably failing to acknowledge the real complexity and difficulty of the issues at stake.

Ultimately, it is the notion of "effects" itself that is the most problematic aspect of these debates—and of course it is precisely this notion that continues to inform the vast bulk of research on children and television. To see children's relationship with television solely in terms of its "effects," however, is to assume that it carries the same meaning for all who watch it—that meaning is simply produced as an automatic "response" to a fixed and straightforward "stimulus." Perhaps because of the continuing dominance of the arguments I have mentioned, research on children and television has barely begun to cast off the legacy of behaviorism. This applies as much, I would argue, to research on social learning from television as it does to the more prominent concerns about violence. Television continues to be seen unproblematically as a powerful form of socialization, an external force that "does things" (and of course, mostly bad things) to children's minds. The notion that children might actively construct meanings from what they watch, and that those meanings might be diverse or ambiguous—let alone that socialization itself might be an equally uncertain and contested process—is only now beginning to be recognized (Buckingham, 1993b; Durkin, 1985; Hodge & Tripp, 1986).

TAKING CONTROL

For the reasons I have implied, these discourses about the negative effects of television have a considerable social currency. Taking a critical stance toward television can serve a variety of wider rhetorical functions: it can provide a guarantee of the speaker's moral or social responsibility, and thus represent a claim to a more powerful social position. For example, research has suggested that parents—and particularly middle-class parents—are often keen to condemn the negative influence of television, and to argue for the need to control their children's viewing (Holman & Braithwaite, 1982; Lull, 1982). Being seen to regulate what your children watch is widely taken to be a mark of "good parenting"—and this is seen in turn to be largely the responsibility of mothers. However, there are often considerable disparities between what parents say about these issues and what they actually do in their own homes. Very few parents appear to intervene in their children's viewing to any significant degree; and when they do so, it is often merely in order to impose their own viewing preferences. In my own research, for example, I have found that children often give accounts of disputes over "family viewing" that are diametrically opposed to those of their parents (Buckingham 1993b). Although parents are keen to present themselves as responsible controllers of their children's viewing, their children themselves will tell stories of how they manage to evade or contest their parents' restrictions, and how they can effectively watch what they like—although of course there is likely to be an element of bravado here too.

These disparities can be explained in a variety of ways. It could be that however much we might wish to control our children, the struggle to do so is much harder than we might care to admit—and there is certainly some evidence for this. Equally, however, research has suggested that there is a powerful "social desirability bias" at work here(McLeod & Brown, 1976). Faced with the probing questions of an academic researcher, parents are likely to respond in ways they feel are socially acceptable, and that will help them to present themselves as good, responsible parents. In my own research, this has been particularly manifested in terms of social class, as working-class parents struggle to control the "elaborated" linguistic codes that they perceive to be required, and thus to lay claim to a more powerful social position. Significantly, although it is mothers who appear to be mainly responsible for exerting this control in practice, it is often fathers who have most to say about it.

Of course, these findings point to a more general phenomenon, which is characteristic not merely of talk about television, but of language more broadly. In talking about television, we are actively choosing to define ourselves in specific ways, not merely as viewers, but also in broader social terms—for example, as a particular kind of parent, or in terms of social categories such as (in this case) class or gender. From this perspective, talk is seen not as a straightforward reflection of what individuals think or believe, but as a form of social action, which serves specific social functions and purposes. Discourses about the negative effects of television can thus be seen not merely as statements of individual attitudes or beliefs, but as linguistic resources that are actively *used* for particular ends (Buckingham, 1993b; Edwards & Potter, 1992; Potter & Wetherell, 1987). Although they are not necessarily employed coherently or consistently, they embody powerful "lay theories" about child rearing and child development, which in turn reflect wider moral and political commitments.

In this chapter, however, I want to focus not on parents but on children themselves—whose voices still go largely unheard in these debates. The data here are taken from small-group discussions with children aged between 7 and 12, conducted as part of a much more extensive research project on the theme of "television literacy" (Buckingham, 1993b, 1993c). I want to concentrate on the ways in which children use these discourses about the negative effects of television, and how they position themselves in relation to them. As I attempt to show, their arguments are often highly ambivalent—a phenomenon that suggests a great deal about the uncertain and contested relationships of power between adults and children.

DISPLACING EFFECTS

Arguments about the negative effects of television are, often implicitly, arguments about *other* people. By virtue of the fact that we are making the arguments in the first place, we are implicitly claiming that we ourselves are exempt from such influences, by virtue of our greater maturity or intelligence or rationality. As in the trial of D.H. Lawrence's *Lady Chatterley's Lover*, the primary concern is not that one might be depraved or offended by such material oneself, but that it might fall into the hands of one's wife or one's servants. Thus, it is working class women who have traditionally been seen to be most vulnerable to the effects of television soap operas—a weakness that is seen to derive from their more emotional disposition and their inability to distinguish between fiction and reality (Allen, 1985; Hobson, 1982). Similarly, arguments about the dangers of "violence" in popular literature have been largely motivated by a fear of unrest among urban working-class youth, who are perceived to be less adequately socialized than their middle-class peers (Barker, 1989).

However, it is children who are quintessentially "other," and who have historically been seen to be most at risk. Both in research and in popular debate, children are predominantly defined in terms of what they lack—that is, in terms of their inability (or unwillingness) to conform to adult norms. Vulnerability, ignorance, and irrationality are seen as part of the inherent nature of childhood—and of course one condition of children remaining "other" is that their own perspectives are largely ignored and misrepresented. By and large, it is adults who claim to speak on their behalf and in their interests—and, in the process, to define them in ways that often serve to sustain our own authority. Here again, the anxious calls to preserve childhood innocence barely mask the sense of potential threat to adult power.

The most immediately striking characteristic of children's talk about these issues is that they themselves engage in the same kind of displacement (Buckingham, 1987; Cullingford, 1984). Of course, 10-year-olds will say, "We aren't influenced by what we watch: it's only little kids who copy what they see. We might have done this when we were much younger, but we certainly don't do it now." And yet, when you talk to these little kids the story is the same. There is a kind of infinite regression here, as children at each age claim to have already attained the age of reason some years previously. Here, for example, is Colin, aged 10, discussing the children's cartoon *Thundercats*.[1]

> It's because/little children. Like my mate, his little brother, he's 2 and he watches it. And that's why they don't put nobody getting killed at the end/because they'll be going about, and if somebody hits them or something, they'll be going "I'm gonna kill you" and everything. It will put hate in their hearts. They put something on, 2-year-olds can't watch it, because they do it, things like that.

Interestingly, Colin argues that the producers in this case are too responsible to show the consequences of serious violence—"They don't put

---

[1]Transcription conventions are simplified here to maximize readability. [. . .] denotes material omitted. Slash (/) denotes a pause. Brackets denote interruptions.

nobody getting killed at the end"—for fear of its potential effects. Although he claimed to find the pro-social morality of these cartoons tiresome—comparing them to the "happily ever after" endings of children's fairy tales—he also argued that this was necessary in order to "teach children a lesson." As in many other such instances, "children" are spoken about in the third person, as if the speaker himself were somehow outside this category. In Colin's case, this concern about "children" was part of his projection of an adult, worldly wise (and at times almost cynical) persona, which he sustained throughout our discussion.

The following extract provides a more extended illustration of how these arguments can be mobilized. Here, a mixed group of 9- and 10-year-olds is discussing the Australian soap operas *Neighbours* and *Home and Away*, which were among the most popular programs for this age group at the time:

> *Estella*: The raping, all that stuff, [in *Home and Away*] it's not very good for children to watch.
> *Sayo*: Yeah, that's true. And it's meant to be an Australian film and Australia's meant to be good.
> *Estella*: On *Neighbours* [...] on *Neighbours* they don't have that rude thing in it, you know
> *Dilesh*: Excitement
> *Estella*: They're not being rude. They have excitement. So you're always [looking forward / Every time at the end.
> *Sayo*: [The only rude thing you ever see about is a man with a towel.
> *Eleanor*: But if there's, like there could be somebody the age of 4 or 5 watching *Neighbours* [or 3], and they'll think all of this stuff like attacking and raping, I don't think it's [very good.
> *Estella*: [*But it's not in Neighbours.*
> *Eleanor*: In *Home and Away*
> *Interviewer*: No in *Home and Away*, then, yeah [. . .] So why do you think that's a bad thing, then?
> *Estella*: It's not [really good for children to watch, it's just not the kind of thing that children should watch.
> *John, Dilesh*: [It's too dirty, it's too dirty.
> *Estella*: Some kids just think "oh, that's really clever," like when there's loads of fights, "oh, I should try that," and then after . . .
> *Dilesh*: But they don't actually hit each other. They make sound effects.
> *Estella*: I know, but still but some children think [they're really doing it.
> *Sayo*: [Some people do, you know [And when they cry, that's [*unclear*]

Eleanor. [And they think that's really good to like kill people.
John: Some people watch that, and then do what they do.
Estella: Like in *Batman* when my mum was a little girl, they always used to watch it, and then when Batman like climbs up the wall, they turn the camera like sidewards. And this boy tried it, and he fell down by trying it.
Int. Yeah, yeah.
Sayo. And they turn the camera right to the ground, and showing you walking up, like on the ground.
Estella. Because I've actually seen that, because my uncle did it. He's got a TV camera, and he plugged it into our telly [. . .]
Int. But do you, do you copy things you've seen on TV?
Various. No.
Dilesh. Some things, some good things.
Estella. Some young children do.

The particular concern about *Home and Away*, which surfaced in a number of other discussion groups, was based on a combination of moral disapproval and arguments about imitation. Thus, the program is defined as "rude" and "too dirty," and (more generally) as not "good," both in itself and in terms of its potential influence. Sayo's first comment here is particularly interesting in this respect: although he implicitly acknowledges that he does not have first-hand knowledge of Australia, the program is problematic for him in that it seems to violate a notion of what Australia is "*meant* to be"—a notion that seems to have been constructed largely in other television programs and possibly in tourist publicity as well. By contrast, much of the appeal of *Neighbours* for these children derived not only from its projection of Australia as the "lucky country," but also from its avoidance of the moral complexities and the darker social problems represented in British soaps, which were widely described as "gloomy" and depressing. However, in addition to this generalized moral condemnation, *Home and Away* is also accused of providing instruction for potential rapists and attackers, or at least for encouraging children to believe that violence is somehow "really clever." It is perhaps worth emphasizing here that the children are not discussing Kung Fu movies or the *Terminator* series, but a domestic soap opera in which violence is comparatively rare, and is represented almost exclusively from the perspective of the victims.

At the same time, of course, the children are very interested in the transgressions the program represents—albeit ones that to most adult eyes are probably very mild. Elsewhere in this and other discussions, they debated the behavior of particular characters and the evolution of the storylines in considerable detail, suggesting rather more than an occasional acquaintance with the program. However, this apparent inconsistency is rationalized here by constructing a group of "other people," who in this instance are seen to be incapable of distinguishing between fiction and reality, and thus to be "at risk" from the text in a way that they themselves claim not to be. Thus, although they are keen to display their knowledge that the program is not real—and in fact went on to a lengthy discussion of special effects—this level of protective expertise is seen, by definition, not to be available to all. Estella's anecdote about *Batman* is a variant of what amounts to a popular mythology about the effects of television, which is replete with hearsay accounts of children who have jumped out of windows after watching *Superman*. These "others" are defined in various ways as the discussion proceeds, both vaguely ("some people" and "some children") and in more concrete terms ("somebody the age of 4 or 5," or the boy in Estella's anecdote about *Batman*). As in the first extract, the children here attempt to exempt themselves from the category of "young children," defined as being at a safe chronological distance from their own age—although certainly in some of Estella's contributions, there is a sense in which "children" in general are somehow defined as "other."

THE PARENTAL VOICE

On one level, of course, we might well suspect that these children are simply rehearsing arguments they have heard their parents make, perhaps on many occasions: aside from Estella's anecdote, which derives from her mother, a phrase like "not the kind of thing that children should watch" betrays a tone that might reasonably be called parental. In their accounts of "family viewing," the children themselves quoted numerous instances of this kind of parental intervention, although their responses to this were quite diverse. In the case of Jasmine and Nicola (aged 7), for example, their mothers' arguments appeared to be largely accepted. Although they were prepared to accept that *Neighbours* might be appropriate for children, the same was not true of *Home and Away.*

> *Interviewer.* Why do you say *Home and Away* is not for children?
> *Jasmine.* Because/it's like when Bobby lost her mind and um it's sort of things and drugs and sort of wine and everything, and it's going to encourage children to do that when they get older. [. . .] I think it should be a 15 program, 'cause it's got lots of things that children shouldn't see, and it will encourage children to do all that, [so it
> *Nicola.* [I think it should be at 10 o'clock.
> *Jasmine.* Yeah.
> *Int.* But do you think it encourages you?

Nicola: No, I don't really watch it. [People just tell/people just *Jasmine:* [I don't watch it./I don't really watch it either. I don't watch it at all. People just tell me what happens in it, and I don't really think it's suitable for children. I think *Neighbours* is all right, a bit of violence in it, but, that's all right, just a bit of arguing.

As in the previous dialogue, the girls combine concerns about morality with arguments about imitation. Here again, the principal focus is on the potential effects on "children," defined here in general terms, but also in the third person ("when *they* get older"). Significantly, the girls attempt to exempt themselves from this category by claiming that they personally do not watch the program, and that their evidence about it is based on hearsay—although it is notable that Jasmine refers to a character in the program by name, which might suggest a more direct familiarity with it. Both argue for the need for censorship by the broadcasters themselves—although in fact the classification system (as in Jasmine's notion of a "15 program") only applies to films and videotapes.[2] Nevertheless, both arguments here are based on implicit norms of "good parenting" and child development, which would be concerned to ensure that children are in bed by a certain time and that they are not exposed to "unsuitable" material.

In rehearsing these arguments, Jasmine and Nicola appear implicitly to trust their parents to make decisions on their behalf, and to act in their best interests. In fact, however, Jasmine's accounts of the arguments and debates that took place around her family television set suggested that she was very far from passively compliant with her parents' authority: she offered a number of humorous anecdotes, in which she played one parent off against the other, or pestered and blackmailed them until they broke down and gave in to her demands. "Family viewing" appeared to be characterized, not by harmony, but by a constant struggle for control.

However, there were many other instances in which the rights of parents were challenged, both implicitly and explicitly. In general, such parental arguments were reported with a considerable degree of irony, as in the following extract, which features two 7-year-old cousins:

---

[2] Nicola's comment here may refer to the convention of the "watershed" in British broadcasting, whereby programs deemed unsuitable for family viewing should only be shown after 9 o'clock.

Interviewer: So are there programs you're not allowed to watch?

Sasha: Like um films and stuff. I wanted to watch *Home and Away* and she said, "It's not GOOD for you to watch."

Int: *Home and Away* is not good for you to watch, why's that?

Sasha: I don't know, 'cause it's got all kind of stuff, kissing and all that. [. . .] And sometimes with films that swear, when I hear the swearing bit she says [mock-child voice:] "Sasha, you're not supposed to be watching that, and you, Chanel, I'll smack both of your bottoms!"

Chanel: And if we sit next to the, closer to the television, she goes "don't sit next to the television so close, 'cause you're going to get bad eyes, you're going to have to wear glasses."

The tone of mockery here is characteristic of a number of these discussions. Parents' views about the effects of television, and their attempts to protect their children from aspects of the world of which they were assumed to be innocent, were often parodied, amid considerable amounts of laughter. Sasha's assumption of a child-like voice (again, not uncommon in reporting the views of parents) suggests that her mother's arguments are seen as appropriate to a child much younger than herself. For Sasha and Chanel, as for many other children in our sample, these strictures were merely one of the more absurd dimensions of adult authority: they represented something to be avoided, in the same way as household chores or other irritating adult demands.

It must be said, however, that this applied much more to representations of sex (as in this case) than of violence. Although there were occasional expressions of enthusiasm for violent material, and some self-consciously bloodthirsty accounts of horror movies, few of the children were ready to make a case for the positive benefits of viewing violence. Indeed, the abstract term "violence" itself, which occurs in Jasmine's comments on *Neighbours*, was nearly always used pejoratively, and often seemed to derive from the kind of parental discourses I have been describing. (It is notable, for example, that Jasmine appears to define "arguing" as a form of "violence," which suggests that it is rather an elastic category for her.) Clearly, both parents and children may experience considerable embarrassment at watching scenes of sexual behavior in each other's company, and "moral" arguments may be mobilized in order to prevent this happening. However, the notion that children somehow do not know about these things—and, more significantly, should not be allowed to find out about them—was often challenged. Hayley, aged 10, offered one account of this kind of debate:

Hayley: Well, I'm not allowed to watch ["rude" programs]. My mum doesn't like me watching them, 'cause she doesn't think it's right. And people wearing like /um/ sort of like this, you know with Alexis and

Interviewer: *Dynasty*?

Hayley: Yeah, *Dynasty*. You know when they get into bed and they have a little cuddle and all that, [my mum doesn't think that

Int: [laughing:] She's always getting into bed and having little cuddles, in my memory!

Hayley: Um, my mum doesn't like me watching those things, she doesn't think it's right. She goes, "When you're 18, stuff like that, you can start watching that stuff, 'cause you might be doing it soon." [laughs]

Int: And what do you think of her?

Hayley: She's horrible.

Int: Your mum [laughs] not letting you watch it?

Hayley: I like it, it's funny. Usually if she does send me out of the room, she goes, "Go upstairs to your room" and what I usually do is I creep into the front room and watch it / and when I hear her open the door I quickly turn it off and I quickly sort of like, I stand at the door, going, I get out my homework, and I'm sitting on the floor doing my homework.

Hayley's account of how she resists her mother's attempts at regulation is characteristic of many of the children we interviewed, as is her use of homework as the perfect alibi. Particularly in larger families, and those with access to more television sets, the opportunities for parental control are significantly reduced. Hayley was by no means the only child who described how she would avoid her parents' attempts to prevent her from viewing by simply going to watch on another set elsewhere in the house. This kind of guerrilla war over television—and particularly over "forbidden" material—appeared to be a recurrent feature of family life.

Like many of the girls (and predictably few of the boys), Hayley is not unwilling to admit to an interest in "kissing" and "little cuddles"— although, as the laughter indicates, there was inevitably a certain amount of mutual embarrassment here. Here again, the argument about what is appropriate for children to watch rests on assumptions about child development, although Hayley herself explicitly mocks and rejects these. By describing the sex in *Dynasty* as "funny," she implicitly positions herself as more distanced and mature, and hence as somehow immune from dangerous moral effects.

As these extracts suggest, children may use parental discourses about the negative influence of television in quite ambivalent ways. In the majority of instances in this discussion, these arguments were parodied or directly rejected—and in this respect, Hayley's comments are much more typical than those of the children quoted earlier. Even where they appear to accept and reproduce the arguments, as in the case of Jasmine, their reports of their own behavior often appear to conflict with this. It would seem that although parental authority may be seen as correct in principle (significantly, of course, in the context of an interview with an adult), it may be much harder to accept in practice.

DEFINING THE SELF

As I have implied, children's discussions of the effects of television necessarily involve them in constructing "subject positions" from which they are seen to speak—positions that are defined largely in terms of age. In condemning the negative effects of television—which they do primarily in relation to violence—the children often seem to imply that they themselves are immune from them. "Children"—and particularly "little children"—may be at risk, but they themselves are somehow excluded from this category. In adopting the parental voice, they implicitly claim a form of maturity; in parodying it, they also appear to be rejecting the position of the "child" that is inscribed within it.

This attempt to renegotiate the respective positions of "child" and "adult" is characteristic of a great deal of children's talk about television (Buckingham, 1994). The considerable peer group status of horror videos, for example, clearly derives at least partly from the fact that children are legally forbidden to watch them. To claim that one watches such films—and, more particularly, that one isn't scared by them—represents a powerful claim to adult status. In these discussions, many children were keen to offer accounts of such films, even ones they had not actually seen themselves. By contrast, "owning up" to liking programs that were perceived as "babyish" was much more problematic—although some of the older girls did manage to accomplish this, albeit with a kind of nostalgic irony. However, this kind of aspirational talk is manifested, not merely in the preferences children proclaim, but also in the discourses they employ in describing them. In this context, the act of adopting a "critical" discourse about television—for example, in condemning programs as "unrealistic" or stereotyped—can serve as a powerful guarantee of the speaker's adult sophistication. It must be seen, not merely as evidence of children's cognitive abilities, but as a claim for social status that needs to be situated in the interpersonal context in which it is performed.

However, age may also interact with other factors, as the following example suggests. Here, Jennifer and Alice, two 10-year-olds, are discussing *Brave Starr*, a science-fiction cartoon. Although Alice does express some enthusiasm for the program, the discussion quickly comes to focus on its shortcomings. Although both girls have clearly seen the program many times—they are able to repeat the songs and catch phrases—they are keen to condemn it as unrealistic, predictable, and corny. Of course, there is a sense in which the program is a very easy target for these kinds of judgments. Elsewhere in the discussion, the girls proclaim a preference for programs like *Doctor Who* and *Batman* and films like *Superman* and *Alice In Wonderland*, which would imply that their preferences are not necessarily guided by considerations about what is "lifelike."

In fact, it becomes clear from the remainder of their discussion that the motivation for Alice and Jennifer's critique of *Brave Starr* derives largely from the social interaction which frames the viewing context. Jennifer introduces the program into the discussion by complaining that her older brother insists on watching it when she wants to watch *Blue Peter*. Alice goes on to describe how her younger cousin makes her watch it when she visits their house, despite her attempts to go elsewhere and watch a "good video." Both girls claim that they don't like the fighting in the program, and Jennifer suggests that "it encourages people to fight," a point which Alice develops in the following extract:

> *Interviewer:* But you're saying you think it encourages people to fight, yeah?
> *Alice:* Mmm. 'Cause [it does.
> *Jennifer:* ['Cause it is always fighting, like the *A-Team* and that, like we were talking about last time.
> *Alice:* When I was 6, / my cousin was quite young, he was only about 10 or 11, and he um / he didn't watch *Brave Starr* and he was rather gentle /
> *Jennifer:* I thought *Brave Starr* wasn't on then.
> *Alice:* Yeah. And he was, he didn't have it in Cheshire, you see. And so, and then *Brave Starr* just started when he was about 7.
> *Jennifer:* It didn't, it only started about a month ago [laughs].
> *Alice:* It started ages ago, I mean. But / it, when he started watching it, when he was 16, he always bullies me, because, I think it's because of *Brave Starr* and all the *A- Team* programs that he watches. 'Cause he just, I mean, when he
> *Jennifer:* At 16 or 17, in their teens, they always think they're so big and stuff.
> *Alice:* I know, like
> *Jennifer:* Like my brother [. . .]
> *Int:* So you're thinking he's become a bit of a bully, then, because of [the TV?
> *Alice:* [Yeah, he's also very babyish. 'Cause I thought, I mean, I watched it a long time ago, / I did, I watched it, but then I went

off it, 'cause I thought, this is stupid, it is just so babyish. /
'Cause it is. I mean it's meant to be violent, for all ages, but it's
not! It's for little toddlers, 'cause they think
Jennifer: It's not for toddlers, it teaches them bad manners!
Alice: I know / They think it is for toddlers, you see. So I went
out of it / really long time ago now.

Here, the critique of *Brave Starr* is extended through arguments
about "effects," both of a general nature—for example, Jennifer's distinct-
ly "parental" comment about "bad manners"—and in the form of Alice's
specific "case study" of her older cousin. Although Jennifer questions the
detail of Alice's assertions here—the chronology is certainly confused!—
the girls are united in their attempt to define the program's audience as
"other" than themselves. This has a number of dimensions. Gender is certainly at stake here: "bullying" and "fighting" are clearly seen as things that
boys do, and the word "they" is, I would argue, implicitly male throughout.
Nevertheless, later in the discussion, Alice directly refuted the male interviewer's suggestion that *Brave Starr* was "for boys," referring to the fact that
her younger cousin, who is a girl, is also a fan of the program—as, of
course, she admits to being herself, at least when younger. Age is also an
issue, although again this is complicated. Alice defines her older cousin as
"babyish"—reflecting a familiar complaint among girls about boys' "imma-
turity" (a complaint that was rarely made the other way around). Similarly,
although it is possible for her to admit to some previous enthusiasm for
the program, this is situated well in the past, a "really long time ago."
Finally, although they are omitted here, there are recurrent references in
this discussion that serve to situate the girls in terms of social class: Alice
talks about her cousins' "massive" country house with its "TV in every
room," whereas Jennifer claims that her own house is equally "massive"—
thereby marking their difference from the other children in their class at
school, whose domestic circumstances are considerably more deprived.

In general, therefore, it would seem that the girls' critique of the
program is, in effect, a critique of its viewers: indeed, the crucial word
"babyish" is applied to both. Defining who the program is "for"—as they
attempt to do, amid some confusion, at the end of this extract—is in this
respect their main concern (and there are notable similarities here with
Jasmine and Nicola's comments on the audience for the Australian
soaps). In distinguishing themselves from these "others," the girls are also
defining themselves: their critique of the "unrealistic" nature of the program, combined with related arguments about "effects," enables them to
build a mutually acceptable definition of their identity, in terms of gender, social class and overall "maturity". Given the vulnerability of their target, this is an achievement they are able to manage with comparative ease.

CONFESSION TIME

Clearly, the interview context is not a neutral one in this respect. Any adult asking children questions about television, particularly in the context of a school, is likely to "cue" these discourses about the negative effects of the medium. Children know very well that most adults disapprove of them watching "too much" television—or certain kinds of television—and in this respect our motivations as researchers must inevitably give them cause for suspicion. Although they may well seek to disabuse us of the falsity of these ideas (at least in relation to them personally), they are likely to perceive the context as one in which these kinds of discourses are at least appropriate, if not positively required. Of course, children may not always choose to play what they perceive to be the interviewer's game; but we should certainly be wary of taking what they say at face value, as though it were some kind of neutral reflection of their attitudes or beliefs (Buckingham 1993b).

As I have noted, children generally attempted to displace these arguments about "effects" on to other people, particularly those younger than themselves. However, there were a few instances of a more "confessional" approach, as in the following extract. Here, three 10-year-olds are discussing *The A-Team*—a program that in Britain has become almost synonymous with arguments about the negative effects of television.[3]

> *Interviewer:* So what do you think about [*The A-Team*], then?
> *Hussein:* I think that it's [good], but the thing I don't like about it, it's got a bit too much violence.
> *Int:* So why don't you like violence, then?
> *Hussein:* Because, um, a number of children as they watch the, um, violent films, they get the habit of doing it at certain places.
> *Int:* Mmm /
> *Hussein:* So sometimes when I watch *The A-Team*, and after I've watched *The A-Team*, and a couple of days after I start to get a bit violent.
> *Int:* Mhm. So what sort of things d' you do, then?
> *Hussein:* I get, I go in my room and I start building things from Lego and everything and start attacking my brother. [Interviewer laughs] It is kind of funny, but it causes a big fight after.
> *Int:* And that's because you watch *The A-Team?*

---

[3]It was, for example, the single program named by the incoming Chairman of the Broadcasting Standards Council, Lord Rees-Mogg, as the one he would like to see banned from British screens.

Hussein: Yeah, sometimes.
Int: What, so what's *The A-Team* got to do with that? I mean, do you?
Hussein: No, I get this kind of feeling that why don't I have a go at doing it, it might, it might happen, so I do it on my brother, and we start getting violent.

Coming at the very beginning of the discussion, Hussein's "confession" may well have reflected his attempt to guess at the "hidden agenda" of the research, even though such issues had not been mentioned. As noted earlier, the use of the comparatively abstract term "violence" (repeated several times) may be significant here; and, as in previous extracts, Hussein also begins with the generalized notion of "children." Nevertheless, his account of the way in which these "effects" apparently occurred is rather vague. Hussein may well get into fights with his brother, but his attempts to blame this on *The A-Team* are somewhat equivocal—the fights occur "a couple of days after," "it is kind of funny," and it only happens "sometimes."

It emerged later in the discussion that the source of this discourse was in fact television itself: Hussein referred to a program which seems to have included an experiment in which children were forced to do without violent television, and apparently became less violent as a result. Indeed, this program in fact included a sequence in which a teenager described how television had made him violent—and this was also recalled by a child in another of our discussion groups. Hussein's "confession" may possibly represent an attempt to echo this.

However, there was also a considerable degree of irony and humor in Hussein's accounts of the "effects" of television. The following extract, taken from later in the same discussion, is a particularly choice example on which to conclude:

Obinna: My mum doesn't like me seeing those rude bits. [laughter]
Interviewer: Rude bits. So what do you mean by rude bits, like language, or?
Hussein: My mum don't look, you know, when
Jennifer: All those love films [laughs]
Hussein: All the love films when they you know [Jennifer laughs] My mum don't, when the film starts yeah, my mum says, "Do you want to watch TV?" I go "yeah," and so I sit down, yeah, and I don't know what the TV, I don't know what the program is, so I just watch it and I realize it's a dirty film, so when a dirty bit comes my mum goes "close your eyes" [laughter]. And I get a pillow and I just slam it onto my er / face [laughter].

Jennifer: And then you peep [laughs]
Hussein: And then um I feel like peeping.
Obinna: That's what I do.
Jennifer: I go like this [mimes]
Hussein: I feel like peeping, but then I, you know when, one block, this side of my head says, it's the devil's bit, it says, "Go on, peep, peep, nothing's gonna happen to you" and everybody says, "No, it's dirty, don't look at it, it's naughty." And then I go, and then um, / and then I go, "I might as well look, yeah, cause it is gonna finish in a little while," so I just move a little bit and I started looking. [Jennifer laughs loudly] Like, and then this side, um the good part of my brain goes, "Oh no!"
Jennifer: What, does it say "I'm not your friend now, I'm going to tell on you" [laughs]
Hussein: No, and the devil's bit, you know, I just look at it and then I just remember it, and when I look at it it's two dogs um / and the devil punches the fairy on the nose and he falls down the cloud and he goes ha ha ha ha and I just start looking [at] it.

If we take Hussein's comments in these two extracts literally, we might say that he displays an extraordinary degree of self-awareness about his own mental processes—a quality that psychologists would call *metacognition*. In the first extract, he appears to be able to trace the causes of his behavior in terms of his prior exposure to a violent stimulus—albeit several days earlier, and despite the considerable differences between the scenarios of *The A-Team* and the act of fighting in the bedroom with pieces of Lego. In the second, he aptly conveys the combination of fascination and moral disapproval with which he watches these programs—although, as in Hayley's case, his mother's strictures may simply reflect a desire to avoid mutual embarrassment. Nevertheless, Hussein's comments reflect some quite elaborate commonsense psychological theories, for example about social learning and morality (Furnham, 1986).

To describe his comments in these terms, however, as manifestations of "pure" cognition, is to ignore the significance of the social context in which they occur. As I have implied, the "confession" in the first extract may well have been fabricated in order to give the interviewer what he is perceived to want—and despite the interviewer's somewhat skeptical questions, it is intended to be taken seriously. By contrast, in the second extract the account is characterized by a considerable degree of humor. As I have noted, the children's arguments about the effects of sexual material are significantly different from their arguments about violence, and this partly accounts for the differences between these two extracts. However, Hussein's description of his moral dilemmas here is conveyed in highly exaggerated, stereotypical terms, as a matter of fairies wrestling with devils. It is clearly delivered for an audience, and with a kind of self-deprecating irony, in which Jennifer also participates. One might almost say that it satirizes the conventional ways in which mental processes tend to be described, and with them some of the more absurd formulations of the "effects" discourse.

CONCLUSION

My aim in this chapter has been to analyze some of the ways in which children typically describe the negative "effects" of television. In adopting approaches derived from discourse analysis, I have sought to identify some of the contradictions and inconsistencies that characterize these discussions, as well as the social purposes that are at stake. In talking about such "effects," children are not simply offering straightforward accounts of their own attitudes or experiences; nor are they simply rehearsing opinions they have derived from elsewhere. As I have argued, talk about television represents a form of social action in which we proclaim and negotiate our social identities. This is a process that is necessarily characterized by irony and ambiguity, and whose complexity we must acknowledge and respect.

This approach has broader implications in terms of research on children and television. In terms of methodology, it means that we cannot afford to take what children say at face value—whether in the context of an open-ended discussion of the kind reported here, or indeed of a questionnaire or a laboratory experiment. We need to regard discourse as necessarily inconsistent and provisional—and, more crucially, as inherently social. This means that traditional psychological notions of "attitude" and "belief," on which research into children's social learning from television has largely been based, need to be seriously questioned—as indeed they are increasingly being in other areas of social and psychological research (Potter & Wetherell, 1987).

Finally, where does this leave the notion of "effects"? In questioning the ways in which this idea is used, it has not been my intention merely to suggest that television has no effects, or even that it has only beneficial effects. On the contrary, my argument is that the notion of "cause and effect" is itself a particular discursive construction, which in turn serves particular social purposes. In the kinds of discussions I have been analyzing here, it is often used to support children's attempts to lay claim to "adult" status, or otherwise to distance themselves from what are seen to be "childish" inadequacies. As I have shown, these attempts are inevitably fraught with difficulties and contradictions. Aside from the odd "confession," "effects" are largely seen to be something from which other people suffer; and in distinguishing themselves from those other people, both children and adults are seeking primarily to define themselves.

In the context of research, however, the notion of "effects" has often served to justify theoretical assumptions and methodological practices that are all too often taken for granted. In this respect, mainstream research on children and television has remained largely insulated from the broader challenges that have changed the whole landscape of the human sciences over the past two decades (Luke, 1990; Rowland 1983). Both in research and in public debate, the argument about the effects of television has repeatedly come down to a set of either/or choices: either television is bad for children, or it is good for them. Yet it is precisely these narrow, either/or choices that we need to move beyond. In the end, it makes little sense to ask or answer such questions in general terms, and in isolation from the range of other social forces and relationships of which television is merely a part.

REFERENCES

Allen, R.C. (1985). *Speaking of soap opera.* Chapel Hill: University of North Carolina Press.

Barker, M. (1989). *Comics: Ideology, power and the critics.* Manchester, England: Manchester University Press.

Buckingham, D. (1987). *Public secrets: "EastEnders" and its audience.* London: British Film Institute.

Buckingham, D. (1993a). Introduction: Young people and the media. In D. Buckingham (Ed.), *Reading audiences: Young people and the media* (pp. 1-23). Manchester, England: Manchester University Press.

Buckingham, D. (1993b). *Children talking television: The making of television literacy.* London: Falmer.

Buckingham, D. (Ed.). (1993c). *Reading audiences: Young people and the media.* Manchester, England Manchester University Press.

Buckingham, D. (1994). Television and the definition of childhood. In B. Mayall (Ed.), *Children's childhoods observed and experienced* (pp. 79-96). London: Falmer.

Connell, I. (1984). Fabulous powers: Blaming the media. In L. Masterman (Ed.), *Television mythologies* (pp. 88-93). London: Comedia.

Cullingford, C. (1984). *Children and television.* Aldershot: Gower.

Durkin, K. (1985). *Television, sex roles and children.* Milton Keynes: Open University Press.

Edwards, D., & Potter, J. (1992). *Discursive psychology.* London: Sage.

Furnham, A. (1986). *Lay theories.* Oxford: Pergamon.

Hobson, D. (1982). *Crossroads: The drama of a soap opera.* London: Methuen.

Hodge, B., & Tripp, D. (1986). *Children and television: A semiotic approach.* Cambridge: Polity.

Holman, J., & Braithwaite, V.A. (1982). Parental lifestyles and children's television viewing. *Australian Journal of Psychology, 34*(3), 375-82

Luke, C. (1990). *Constructing the child viewer: A history of the American discourse on television and children, 1950-1980.* New York: Praeger.

Lull, J. (1982). The social uses of television. In C. Whitney, E. Wartella, & S. Windahl (Eds.), *Mass communication review yearbook* (Vol. 3, pp. 397-410). Beverly Hills: Sage.

Lusted, D. (1985). A history of suspicion: Educational attitudes to television. In D. Lusted & P. Drummond (Eds.), *TV and schooling* (pp. 11-18). London: British Film Institute.

McLeod, J., & Brown, J.D. (1976). The family environment and adolescent television use. In R. Brown (Ed.), *Children and television* (pp. 199-233). London: Collier MacMillan.

Pearson, A. (1984). Falling standards: A short, sharp history of moral decline. In M. Barker (Ed.), *The video nasties* (pp. 88-103). London: Pluto.

Potter, J. & Wetherell, M. (1987). *Discourse and social psychology: Beyond attitudes and behaviour.* London: Sage.

Rowland, W. (1983). *The politics of television violence.* Beverly Hills, CA: Sage.

3

Television and Persistence

Robin Flanagan
John B. Black
Columbia University

Television viewing has been blamed for numerous social and educational problems (see, for example, Healy, 1990; Mander, 1978; Postman, 1985; Winn, 1977). Most disturbing are concerns that television viewing may be causing behavioral problems such as poor concentration, poor persistence, and high restlessness. For the most part, attempts to identify a relationship between television and any of these ills have shown mixed results, or have provided only anecdotal evidence. Typically, television research has attempted to identify a single factor of television programming that could account for behavioral problems for two reasons: it is good science to identify specific factors that cause the phenomenon of concern, and presumably if the factor could be identified the problem could be fixed. Factors examined include program pace, prosocial or antisocial message, or action-type content (Anderson & Collins, 1988; Anderson, Levin, & Lorch, 1977; Friedrich & Stein, 1973; Singer, Singer, & Rapaczynski, 1984; Tower, Singer, Singer, & Biggs, 1979).

We are concerned that problems such as persistence may not be a matter of poor television programming but may have more to do with the television viewing experience itself. Clark (1983) has argued articulately that when a mediated learning experience and a nonmediated learning experience are made equivalent in every factor save the one under consideration any apparent medium effect disappears. However, Kozma (1991) has pointed out that although there may be no medium effect when mediated and nonmediated experiences are equivalent, educational media certainly tend to facilitate qualitatively different types of learning situations. We propose that television viewing facilitates a learning situation in which the learner is passive and the learner's actions are unrelated to the feedback and stimulation the learner receives. We propose that the behavioral problems associated with television viewing may be a form of learned helplessness and may therefore be best understood within the context of learned helplessness research. Television is a learning environment within which what the viewer experiences (and learns) has nothing to do with what the viewer does, and this lack of contingency is what characterizes learned helplessness. Thus conditions sufficient for learned helplessness are induced whenever the television set is switched on.

In this chapter we examine the relationship between television and persistence based on literature from within television research as well as from learned helplessness research. We argue that looking at single elements of television programming which might affect persistence is not enough to understand this complex medium and its impact on the viewer. Instead, we believe that the effect of television viewing is best understood in terms of the learning environment facilitated by the medium, and it is this learning environment that must be examined for effects. Learning and memory research made a profound transition a few decades ago when it shifted from considering single elements of the environmental stimuli to considering the cognitive processing and internal representations involved in learning and memory. We feel that a similar shift needs to occur in media research in order to more fully comprehend what the mediated learning experience involves.

IN SEARCH OF THE MEDIUM EFFECT

Traditionally, television research has attempted to identify aspects of television programming that could account for television effects. That is, comparisons are made between groups exposed to one type of television program and groups exposed to another type of television program. In each of these studies some aspect of persistence was examined following some form of television viewing experience. For the purposes of this chapter, we define persistent behaviors as behaviors that increase attention to task, length of time on task, ability to ignore distraction, and ability to continue a task that the child finds difficult.

Several studies have looked at television programming factors, such as program pace, on persistence. For example, Anderson et al. (1977) constructed slow-paced and fast-paced versions of *Sesame Street* by splicing together slow- and fast-paced segments of existing episodes. Seventy-two 4-year-olds were assigned to three groups: one watched the fast-paced version, one watched the slow paced version and one listened to a parent read a story. After 40 minutes of experiencing one of the three medium conditions the children were tested on making impulsive choices, and on the amount of time they spent working on a puzzle task.

Finally, they were observed during free play for the length of time they stayed with a toy, and how directed the child's play was. No difference was found between the groups on any of the measures except the number of times the child looked away from the puzzle task. On this measure the children watching the slow-paced television program looked away significantly more often than did children in the other two groups. Although this is a good demonstration that program pace itself does not negatively affect persistence, we think it is important to note that all three conditions provided passive learning experiences with no direct participation. The most involved situation was, of course, the one in which the child's parent reads a story. In this condition the child's experience depends somewhat on factors such as maintaining a relationship with the parent, negotiating a reading relationship, such as being close enough to hear or asking the parent to read more loudly. Clearly, however, these differences were not sufficiently great to show up in this study.

Tower et al. (1979) studied 58 4-year-olds for 10 days. One group watched *Sesame Street* (a fast-paced television program), one group watched *Mister Rogers* (a slow-paced television program), and one group watched educational films. They measured the child's concentration during play, which they operationally defined as the extent to which the child remained with an activity and resisted distraction. They measured the imaginativeness of the children by observing to what extent their play transcended the constraints of reality There were no differences by experimental condition, but there was a difference based on the imaginativeness measure. They found a slight but insignificant decrease in concentration for children with high imagination, and found a slight increase in concentration for those children with low imagination. These differences were across condition. There were no significant differences among groups on this measure. *Sesame Street* and *Mister Rogers* are different types of program in many ways, but it is hard to see any way in which they differ from each other that they do not differ equally from educational films. Again we think that these three conditions do not differ as learning situations from each other in any remarkable way. None of the conditions provides an active role for the learner and none provides an opportunity for contingent feedback.

Singer et al. (1984) undertook a longitudinal study over 5 years with 63 children. They found an effect of television program type on restlessness. This study is noteworthy in its attempt to look at long-term effects and in its use of an indirect measure of restlessness. Many other factors of the study, however, are based on self-reports by the children's parents and must be interpreted with this limitation in mind.

In this study, parents kept intermittent diaries of television viewing behavior for 2 weeks at a time. Midway through the study the experimenters interviewed the parents and children. The parents were asked to answer questions about daily routine in the home, style of discipline, television use in the home (such as viewing rules, number of television sets, specialized cable services) and questions about the child's typical behavior. The children were tested and interviewed for IQ, cognitive skills, and knowledge of television characters.

At the end of the study, the children completed a questionnaire about how scary the world was, and they were also observed for restlessness in the waiting room. An observer watched the child as he or she waited 5 minutes for the interview to begin, and noted signs of restlessness, such as rapid movements, demands for attention, aimless motor activity, and annoyance at waiting. They found that restlessness was positively associated with IQ, parent-described television environment, and amount of realistic action television viewed based on the television diaries. These researchers felt that the rapid-action images, exciting music, and sound effects might be leading to an inability to tolerate delay in "the nontelevision or 'real world'" (Singer et al., 1984, p. 76). However, other interpretations are possible and this type of viewing choice may be the result of an unexamined factor with which it correlates.

Friedrich and Stein (1973) found differences in various persistent behaviors based on television program type as well. They studied 3 groups of preschoolers who viewed 12 television programs over 4 weeks. Group 1 watched *Batman* (an aggressive television program), group 2 watched *Mister Rogers* (a prosocial television program), and group 3 watched a mix of children's television programs with no aggressive or prosocial message. Children were observed in their classrooms for (a) persistence in carrying out assigned tasks, (b) persistence during free play, (c) tolerance of delay. Friedrich and Stein found an increase in tolerance of delay for groups 2 and 3 (*Mister Rogers* and the mixed programs). They found a decrease in tolerance of delay for group 1 (*Batman*). They found a decrease in persistence in carrying out assigned tasks and during free play for group 1 (*Batman*) only for children of high intelligence; and an increase in persistence in carrying out assigned tasks and during free play for group 2 (*Mister Rogers*) but again only for children of high intelligence. However, it is important to note that all three "learning environments" are very similar. We also think it is possible that if a decrease in persistence is inherent in the television viewing experience it may be possible to counteract it with metacognitive messages, such as those found in many *Mister Rogers* episodes. Some have argued, for example, that changing program content to include more problem solving behavior could have a positive effect on persistence (Rothkopf, 1992).

Some of these studies have found a relationship between some aspect of television programming and persistent behavior following television viewing. Each of the studies found persistent behaviors facilitated by one type of television program over another type (Anderson et al., 1977;

Friedrich & Stein, 1973; Singer et al., 1984), or found no difference among treatment conditions (Anderson et al., 1977; Tower et al., 1979).

We conclude from this that television programming factors seem to have an effect on persistent behaviors but that the effect is not universally positive or negative. Thus, some metacognitive or motivational qualities in some television programs may be affecting persistent behavior following television viewing, but nothing inherent in the television viewing experience itself has been identified in these studies as having an effect on persistence.

THE MEDIATED LEARNING ENVIRONMENT

We turn now to the television viewing experience itself, rather than programming factors. The television viewing experience is characterized by viewer passivity. That is, inherent in the viewing experience is an inability to interact with the events, stimulating, educational or otherwise, that are currently in consciousness. This is very similar to several impoverished conditions cited in the animal learning literature such as Diamond's (1990) impoverished rat paradigm and Held's (1965) yoked-cat paradigm, both of which involved an animal able to perceive a stimulating environment but completely unable to interact with it. That is, regardless of how much the animal moved in space, the animal was considered passive in that it could not interact with the environment.

Anderson (1992; Anderson & Collins, 1988) has argued quite vehemently that children do not appear to be passive when watching television because they frequently move around the room and interact with people and objects in the room while they watch television. We want to make it quite clear that this is not what we mean by an active learning environment. It may be that when the child is not attending to the television screen he or she may be participating in something active, valuable, perhaps social. However, as soon as the child's attention returns to the television screen the child is engaging in an experience in which his or her actions are not connected to what the child experiences. It may help to think of this child as being involved in two learning environments: One, mediated, in which the child is involved whenever he or she is attending to the television set and experiencing the result of the television programming; the other, nonmediated, in which the child is involved whenever he or she is attending to the people and objects in his or her room and involved in any form of interaction with them. The television viewing experience, importantly, remains passive and noncontingent on the child's activity.

Although it may be true that there is no factor unique to television viewing to which we may attribute negative influence on learning, we think it is important to notice how similar the television viewing experience is to other learning environments from the literature. For example, the two animal paradigms cited previously were from impoverishment studies that looked at the effect of impoverished environments on learning and brain development. More importantly for this chapter, however, is the remarkable similarity between the television viewing experience and the uncontrollable environment so central to the learned helplessness literature.

Learned helplessness refers to the debilitated behavior exhibited by people and animals following uncontrollable circumstances, such as uncontrollable loud noise, or an experience in which outcomes are not contingent on the learner's actions. Learned helplessness research began with animals, but learned helplessness research involving humans has rejected the animal data as insufficient to describe the varied responses people make in noncontingent situations. For example, Abramson and her colleagues (Abramson, Seligman, & Teasdale, 1978) reformulated the learned helplessness framework to include three dimensions of attributions people make that helped to explain different reactions to similar circumstances. They claim that the helpless pattern is facilitated by attributions that are internal (pertaining to oneself) rather than external (pertaining to the outside world), and by attributions that are stable (such as IQ) rather than unstable (such as effort), and finally by attributions that are global (pertain to one's whole life) rather than specific (pertain to this particular situation only).

Dweck and her colleagues have studied the learned helplessness pattern and have found that it seems to depend on the type of goals and beliefs the child has.(Diener & Dweck, 1978; Dweck & Leggett, 1988; Elliott & Dweck, 1988). For example, children who approach a task with a learning goal (that is, a goal to learn as much as possible from a task) seem to be able to recover quickly from failure and in fact, often perform better following failure or challenge, while children with a goal to "look good" or to perform well seem to recover slowly if at all from failure or challenge.

Similarly, children who hold the belief that a personal trait, such as intelligence, is malleable, or changeable over time, seem to respond well to challenge or failure, whereas children who believe these same traits to be fixed seem to respond poorly to failure and challenge. This pattern, they found, is both correlational and manipulable. That is, children have general goals and beliefs and these correlate with the learned helplessness pattern. These beliefs and goals, however, can be manipulated experimentally to produce the pattern, regardless of original goals and beliefs.

Although it may be true that people often do make attributions to account for perceived uncontrollability, we feel Abramson et al. (1978) went too far in claiming that "mere exposure to uncontrollability is not sufficient to render an organism helpless; rather, the organism must come to expect that outcomes are uncontrollable in order to exhibit helplessness" (p. 50), and that the data do not bear them out. For example, Oakes and his colleagues (Fox & Oakes, 1984; Oakes, Rosenblum, & Fox, 1982) have studied the learned helplessness pattern in people and in rats. They have found that the pattern does not depend on any particular belief, goal, attitude, or assessment, but simply on receiving feedback that is not contingent on one's actions. Oakes et al. (1982) found that rats which had been given food pellets independent of their behavior performed significantly worse on a lever-press task with food reinforcement than rats that had been given food pellets contingent on nose-poke behavior, and worse than a control group that spent the same amount of time but was not given any food until the end of this phase, even though the three groups of rats received the same amount of food pellets overall. Notice that this is not aversive shock avoidance, or uncontrollability in the face of an unpleasant situation, but mere noncontingency of food delivery.

In a remarkable study, Fox and Oakes (1984) looked at the effect of providing people with contingent or noncontingent feedback. They had subjects play one of two versions of a video game. In one version, targets on the video screen were hit when the player aimed and pressed the game button accurately. In the other version, targets were hit at random, regardless of when the button was pushed. In both versions the targets were hit the same number of times overall. The noncontingent version was constructed so as to give the player the impression that the "hits" followed from the player's actions. Fox and Oakes found that both the contingent and noncontingent players believed the "hits" to be contingent on their actions, even though the hits were in fact only contingent on the actions of the "contingent" group. Following this video game experience, members of the contingent group performed significantly better on a lexical decision task than did the members of the noncontingent group, even though both groups believed that their feedback was contingent on their behavior. Again, notice that this is not an unpleasant situation: both groups are comfortable, playing a game, and achieving some amount of apparent success. The only difference is that one group is having an experience in which their success is not contingent on their actions, even though they believe they are controlling the outcome. Thus, attributions cannot be necessary to produce this effect, nor can feelings of dejection or low self-esteem.

Flanagan (1994), and Flanagan and Black (1994) conducted two studies that focused on mediated versus nonmediated learning environments. In the first study, Flanagan and Black asked two questions. First, would a math class that began with 15 minutes of video-based math instruction produce less persistent behavior than a math class that began with 15 minutes of actively involved math instruction? Second, would overall amount of television viewing be correlated with the child's persistence on hard problems?

Flanagan and Black worked with 61 third graders from three classrooms over four 45 minute sessions. The sessions began with one of two math videos, listening to a math story, or working on tangram puzzles, and were followed by some easy measurement problems and some hard measurement problems. The math videos were produced for PBS by Mathworks and each presented 15 minutes of instruction on one of two topics: scale modeling and doing mental math problems. Both videos embedded instruction within a story framework and included animation, multiple perspectives, and humor. The math story that was read was a story set in ancient China and embedded the mathematical phenomenon of successive doubling within a fairy tale (Pittman, 1986). The researchers edited the story to fit within a 15-minute activity period. The math puzzle was an ancient Chinese puzzle, called the Tangram puzzle, and it involved physically manipulating seven geometric shapes to fit a given puzzle outline. This puzzle could be started by every student regardless of literacy or math skill, but very few could finish the puzzle. It is described in more detail in the second study. The children seemed to enjoy each of these four learning experiences. Each class got all four session types in a different order. The student's persistence was measured by how many clearly marked hard problems they worked on when given a choice. Flanagan and Black found that sessions that began with a passive activity (video viewing or listening to a math story) produced significantly less persistence on hard math problems than sessions that began with a physically interactive activity.

We also attempted to determine how much television they watched at home. This is a notoriously difficult measurement to make (Miller, 1986), especially with young children. We tried two different methods, neither of which correlated significantly with our persistence measure. This may be due to the wide range of reading ability among these students and the heavy reliance of this measurement on reading ability.

Flanagan (1994) did a second study to replicate the finding that as little as 15 minutes of television exposure has an effect on persistence. In this study, she worked with 90 second and third graders from four classrooms of mixed socioeconomic status. Students who missed one of the four sessions were eliminated from the study leaving 77 students: 40 girls and 37 boys, mean age 8.36 years. Of these remaining students 12 were African American, 16 were Hispanic, and 49 were White. Each session began with 15 minutes of either watching an educational video on one of two topics or doing a nonmediated activity on one of those same two topics. Thus each classroom participated in a two-by-two matrix of sessions where video or activity was one dimension and subject matter was the other dimension. The sessions were counterbalanced as to medium and subject matter such that each classroom participated in all four sessions in a different order to balance out practice and exposure effects.

The videos, one on scale modeling and one on doing mental math, were described in the previous study. The activities, also on scale modeling and doing mental math, were as follows. For 15 minutes the students worked on making scale models out of graph paper of one of their school books. For the mental math activity students were led, by the researcher, in practicing a simple mental math technique, as a group, for 15 minutes.

Following the initial 15 minute mediated or nonmediated learning experience the students spent 10 minutes working on Tangram puzzles. Persistence was measured as the number of minutes the student continued to work on a very hard Tangram puzzle before requesting an easier one. This is similar to some other persistence measures that have been used (Banta, 1970), and it has the advantage of cutting across the literacy level and particular math content expertise of the students. The tangram puzzle is an ancient Chinese puzzle using 7 geometric pieces cut from a single square (see Figure 3.1). From these 7 pieces many figures can be made. A puzzle consists of the silhouette of all 7 pieces combined in some way such that all 7 pieces are used and none overlap with each other. A hard puzzle is one in which there are few constraints on where each piece may go but only one combination that works for all pieces (see Figure 3.2, for example). An easy puzzle is one in which the position of one or more pieces is constrained by a unique silhouette (see Figure 3.3).

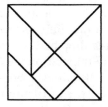

Figure 3.1. Tangram puzzle, 7 pieces from 1 square tile

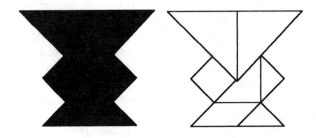

Figure 3.2. A hard tangram puzzle and its solution

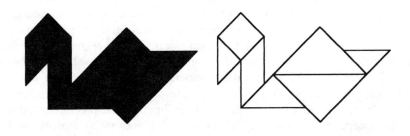

Figure 3.3. An easy tangram puzzle and its solution

At each session, each student was given one of nine different puzzles to work on. No student was given the same puzzle twice and puzzles were assigned randomly, excluding puzzles previously worked on. The students were given 10 minutes at each session to work on them. If students wanted to switch to an easier puzzle they were reminded that there was no trick to the puzzle, it was just a matter of trying a lot of different combinations. If they still wished to switch, they were given an easier puzzle in exchange for the difficult puzzle and a note was made of how many minutes they had worked on the difficult puzzle. Their persistence score was the number of minutes they had worked on the difficult puzzle. Students who worked on the difficult puzzle for the full 10 minutes were given a persistence score of 10 minutes. Students who solved the puzzle were also given a persistence score of 10 minutes.

Flanagan (1994) found that there was a highly significant difference ($F_{1,73}=22.65$, $p < .0001$) between persistence following the video sessions and persistence following the nonmediated sessions such that students persisted on the tangram puzzles longer following the nonmediated sessions (see Figure 3.4). There were no differences between classrooms, between low and high SES, between topics, between boys and girls, between second and third graders, between the two videos, or between the two nonmediated activities.

We feel that, taken together, these studies suggest that perhaps the mere dissociation between the viewer's actions and the feedback received may be inducing a form of learned helplessness in the learner. This view is similar to thoughts put forth by Hearn (1991), who argued that because television provides enjoyable feedback regardless of the viewer's actions, it may be leading to appetitive helplessness. The next section reviews several theories that may help to explain the relationship between television and persistence.

DISCUSSION: A SINGLE ELEMENT

There are several reasons why television might have an effect on persistence in difficult task situations. Three theoretical explanations address specific elements of television programming. First, fast program pace may have an effect on persistence. As Singer et al. (1984) described, the rapid-action images, exciting music, and sound effects might be leading to an

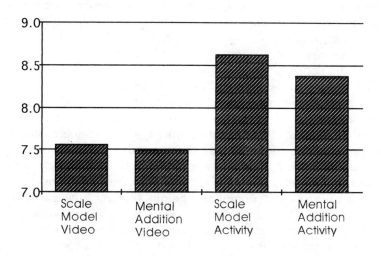

Figure 3.4. Average number of minutes persisted following
mediated or nonmediated learning

inability to tolerate delay in "the nontelevision or 'real' world" (p. 76). However, research on this factor has not supported this explanation or has favored the faster paced program (Anderson et al., 1977; Tower et al., 1979).

Second, television programs contain prosocial or antisocial messages that may affect persistence. This may account for the difference Friedrich and Stein (1973) found, and it may be a mediating factor in other studies as well. For example, the two videos used in the Flanagan and Black studies both contained numerous prosocial and motivational messages that might encourage students to persist longer. If these messages had an effect on persistence, however, it was not sufficient to overcome the effect of the medium itself.

Finally, television's content may omit most effortful or persistent behavior (with the notable exception of car-chase scenes and detective stories), thereby "teaching" through omission that nothing should be hard to solve or require tedious persistence (Rothkopf, 1992). If this is the case, then changing the content of television to include more realistic problem solving and data gathering might change this pattern. Although this is certainly true in part (as noted earlier), inherent in the television programming itself is a focus on polished performance and end product. We can't really expect television to be as tedious, problematic, task oriented, and mundane as ordinary life. Inherent in the medium itself is a dissociation between the actions that lead up to a result and the result itself. Editing, lip-synching, stunt men, special effects, even costumes and make-up combine to make a program event more exciting, entertaining, poignant, or effective. Each of these techniques is designed to make the end product, the television program, better; to enhance it in some way. Even in the rare cases that involve "realistic" or "real life" videos, such as some of the police or rescue shows, some news footage, nature films, or the Loud family of the 1970s PBS series,"An American Family", the people or animals being observed are aware of being observed and may seek to appear to their best advantage (perhaps in subtle ways), or the footage may have been edited or framed specifically for a viewing audience. For example, in nature shows it is rare to see any of the steps that lead up to the amazing nature find that has been videotaped for the television show, and even when these are shown the viewer sees and feels nothing of the weeks or even years of sometimes tedious research that goes into the nature discovery. We watch television precisely because the messy, boring parts have been left out. Therefore, even with the most conscientious of programmers we are left with a medium designed to keep the messy stuff (like problems and effort) behind the scenes while framing and showcasing the end result. In sum, perhaps obviously, television is a performance medium.

THE MEDIATED ENVIRONMENT

We feel that searching for a specific element of television programming to account for behavioral effects such as poor persistence is of limited use. We agree with Clark (1983) that there is little or no medium effect when a single element of the medium is singled out. We also feel that research will be more fruitful in this area if it takes into account the type of learning environment that the medium itself facilitates. We also feel that there are two major reasons that the television medium itself, regardless of specific programming, could be negatively affecting persistent behavior in viewers: The medium could be eliciting attributions about learning from the medium, or the medium could be providing a learning environment in which nothing the viewer does affects anything the viewer experiences. Both of these are forms of learned helplessness, one cognitive and one automatic.

On the one hand, the television learning experience could elicit attributions about the medium. Salomon (1984) argued that the perceived difficulty of a learning medium influences the amount of effort invested in learning from the medium. He further argued that learners who attribute success in learning from a medium to their own effort are more likely to invest effort in learning from that medium. He supports this argument with the results of a study in which he looked at amount of invested mental effort (AIME) in 124 sixth graders watching a silent film or reading a text on similar content. He found that most of the students in the text group attributed their success in learning to internal causes (such as effort) and their failure to the difficulty of the medium, whereas most of the students in the film group attributed their success to the ease of the medium and their failure to internal causes (such as "dumbness" or lack of effort).

Furthermore, he found that 42% of the reading group attributed their success in learning to "effort," whereas only 13% of the silent film group made such an attribution. This is very close to a description of a learned helplessness condition. According to Dweck and colleagues learners who exhibit the learned helplessness pattern make attributions for their success to things like luck and their failure to things like lack of intelligence, whereas those exhibiting a mastery orientation are more likely to attribute their success to effort (Diener & Dweck, 1978, 1980; Dweck & Leggett, 1988; Elliott & Dweck, 1988). If students, during a television learning experience, attribute their success to this easy medium, and their failure to internal causes, as Salomon found with his film group, then this could provide sufficient conditions for learned helplessness to occur. In Flanagan's (1994) study, however, the television learning experience was not rated as significantly easier. This was, however, a crude measurement and this attribution theory is still a possible explanation, awaiting further research.

Finally, television could cause a decrease in persistence as part of a learned helplessness paradigm simply because what the viewer experiences is not contingent on what the viewer does (Hearn, 1991). Related studies have shown this effect in rats doing nose-poke tasks and in humans doing contingent or noncontingent video games (Fox & Oakes 1984; Oakes et al., 1982). According to this theory the conditions for learned helplessness exist as soon as the television set is turned on, regardless of programming.

Specifically, we believe that television, regardless of its content, is setting up a context in which the feedback, stimulation, and rewards that accrue to the viewer are not contingent on what the viewer does, beyond turning the television set on or off, or turning to a different channel. Because of the mere dissociation between action and experience we believe that television viewing provides an environment in which a learned helplessness pattern can emerge. We believe that this is especially dangerous when the viewing experience is labeled "educational." We feel that viewing an educational video is a noncontingent experience, like other television viewing experiences, resulting in a learned helplessness pattern that may continue through other learning experiences. The child, therefore, may or may not be aware of the noncontingency, but in either case the learned helplessness pattern should emerge, leading to decreased persistence and decreased exertion of effort. If the child does form an expectation about the future, which has often been found to be a part of the learned helplessness pattern in humans, it seems likely that it might be something like "learning is easy" or "learning doesn't take any effort or participation on my part" or "if it's hard I'll just turn it off or switch the channel." In short, the viewing of videos labeled in some way as educational may set up a learned helplessness disposition regarding one particular class or topic, regarding one kind of learning, regarding one particular day, or end up feeding a longer term learning disposition that relies heavily on watching, judging, switching when bored, and not making any personal effort.

More research is needed to determine whether this is part of the entire learned helplessness pattern, whether it increases with increased exposure, whether a conscious decision that the learning event should be easy is necessary, or whether mere dissociation of activity and feedback is sufficient, and whether there are ways of framing the television experience so as to diminish this effect. We feel that framing media effects in terms of learned helplessness, as well as in situated or contextual activity, shows great promise and look forward to more research along these lines.

REFERENCES

Abramson, L. Y., Seligman, M. E. P., & Teasdale, J. D. (1978). Learned helplessness in humans: Critique and reformulation. *Journal of Abnormal Psychology, 87*(1), 49–74.

Anderson, D. R. (1992). Television and attention. In C. Clark & K. King (Eds.), *Television and the preparation of the mind for learning: Critical questions on the effects of television on the developing brains of young children* (pp. 57-65). Washington, DC: U.S. Dept. of Health and Human Services Administration for Children and Families.

Anderson, D. R., & Collins, P. A. (1988). *The impact on children's education: Television's influence on cognitive development.* (Working Paper No. 2). Office of Educational Research and Improvement, U.S. Department of Education.

Anderson, D. R., Levin, S. R., & Lorch, E. P. (1977). The effects of TV program pacing on the behavior of preschool children. *AV Communication Review, 25,* 159–166.

Banta, T. J. (1970). Tests for the evaluation of early childhood education: The Cincinnati Autonomy Test Battery (CATB). In J. Hellmuth (Ed.), *Cognitive studies Vol. 1.* New York: Bruner/Mazel.

Clark, R. E. (1983). Reconsidering research on learning from media. *Review of Educational Research, 53*(4), 445–459.

Diamond, M. C. (1990). Morphological cortical changes as a consequence of learning and experience. In A. B. Scheibel & A. F. Wechsler (Eds.), *Neurobiology of higher cognitive function* (pp. 1–12). New York: Guilford.

Diener, C. I., & Dweck, C. S. (1978). An analysis of learned helplessness: Continuous changes in performance, strategy and achievement cognitions following failure. *Journal of Personality and Social Psychology, 36,* 451–462.

Diener, C. I., & Dweck, C. S. (1980). An analysis of learned helplessness II: The processing of success. *Journal of Personality and Social Psychology, 39,* 940–952.

Dweck, C. S., & Leggett, E. L. (1988). A social–cognitive approach to motivation and personality. *Psychological Review, 95*(2), 256–273.

Elliott, E. S., & Dweck, C. S. (1988). Goals: an approach to motivation and achievement. *Journal of Personality and Social Psychology, 54*(1), 5–12.

Flanagan, R. C. (1994). *The effect of mediated vs. non mediated learning on persistence: A study of second and third graders.* Unpublished manuscript, Teachers College, Columbia University.

Flanagan, R. C., & Black, J. B. (1994). *The effect of educational television on persistence in third graders.* Unpublished manuscript, Teachers College, Columbia University.

Fox, P. E., & Oakes, W. F. (1984). Learned helplessness: Noncontingent reinforcement in video game performance produces a decrement in performance on a lexical decision task. *Bulletin of the Psychonomic Society, 22*(2), 113–116.

Friedrich, L. K., & Stein, A. H. (1973). Aggressive and prosocial television programs and the natural behavior of preschool children. *Monographs of the Society for Research in Child Development, 38*(4),1–64.

Healy, J. (1990). *Endangered minds: Children's learning in today's culture.* New York: Simon & Schuster.

Hearn, G. (1991). Entertainment manna: Does television viewing lead to appetitive helplessness? *Psychological Reports, 68,* 1179–1184.

Held, R. (1965). Plasticity in sensory-motor systems. *Scientific American, 213,* 84-94.

Kozma, R. B. (1991). Learning with media. *Review of Educational Research, 61*(2), 179-211.

Mander, J. (1978). *Four arguments for the elimination of television.* New York: Morrow.

Miller, P. V. (1986). *Measuring TV viewing in studies of TV effects.* Paper presented at the annual meeting of the International Communication Association, November, 1986.

Oakes, W. F., Rosenblum, J. L., & Fox, P. E. (1982). "Manna from Heaven": The effect of noncontingent appetitive reinforcers on learning in rats. *Bulletin of the Psychonomic Society, 19*(2), 123–126.

Pittman, H. C. (1986). *A grain of rice.* New York: Bantam.

Postman, N. (1985). *Amusing ourselves to death: Public discourse in the age of show business.* New York: Viking.

Rothkopf, E. Z. (1992, January/February). Cultivating America's gross national intelligence. *CEO/International Strategies,* 68–71.

Salomon, G. (1984). Television is "easy" and print is "tough": The differential investment of effort in learning as a function of perceptions and attributions. *Journal of Educational Psychology, 76*(4), 647–658.

Singer, J. L., Singer, D. G., & Rapaczynski, W. S. (1984). Family patterns and television viewing as predictors of children's beliefs and aggression. *Journal of Communication, 34,* 73–89.

Tower, R., Singer, D., Singer, J., & Biggs, A. (1979). Differential effects of television programming on preschooler's cognition, imagination and social play. *American Journal of Orthopsychiatry, 49,* 265–281.

Winn, M. (1977). *The plug-in drug.* New York: Penguin.

4

Commercial Television and the Limited English Proficient Child: Implications for Language Development

Carla Meskill
University at Albany

There is little doubt that television influences children's knowledge, behavior and attitudes (Wolf, 1987). A recent *Weekly Reader* (1992) survey of elementary students, for example, reveals distinct shifts over the past decade in the degree of children's trust in government. In their attempts to account for this widespread diminution of children's confidence in their political leaders, researchers point to television's high-profile reportage of political scandals as contributing factors. Also, a number of studies on the effects of children's viewing of violent acts on television confirm the suspicion that seeing violence on TV encourages aggressiveness (Gunter, 1985). Likewise, the viewing of prosocial acts on television can affect positive modifications in social behavior (Coates, Pusser, & Goodman, 1976; Friedrich & Stein, 1973) and even increase the likelihood of nonnative speakers of the dominant language becoming more social in the classroom (O'Connor, 1972). These lines of research conclude that children are clearly affected both positively and negatively by television characterizations and that broadcast models of attitudes, behaviors, and actions consciously or unconsciously influence viewers' notions of social appropriateness and ideals. Television models of social behaviors tend to inculcate certain values, instantiate particular behaviors, and nurture specific expectations about life and society.

In terms of the impact these television models affect on viewer communication skills, Traudt and Lont (1987) suggested that television viewing directly contributes to the formation of one's interpersonal habits of communication. Television, they contended, "comes to represent a legitimate model on which to base . . . communication strategies within a host of social settings" (p. 141). Moreover, they believe that viewers selectively use the personalities and related methods of communication of the television characters they watch in their own interpersonal negotiations. This notion of television's influence on social roles and conduct was born out in an ethnographic study of a family's media use. Traudt and Lont found that:

> Television's presentational logic comes to represent a media consciousness on the part of family members . . . this logic comes to represent not only possible sources for social behaviors, but in certain cases, the preferred behaviors for a host of social settings. Family members come to utilize both specific portrayals from television fare and an historical aggregate of these portrayals in order to construct their own identities appropriate to a number of social realms. Television provides a significant resource for the construction of experiences and knowledge regarding one's self, one's role as a family member, and one's role in life outside the home. (p. 159)

Television influences perceptions of the way in which effective transmittal of feelings and information is accomplished. Television can therefore be seen as cultivating children's social reality (Gerbner & Gross, 1976). Models of socially mediated communication pervade television programming and, it can be argued, these pervasive models are both contributing to and/or detracting from the construction of social realities and a concomitant growth of communicative competence in their viewers.

VIEWING LITERACY

It has long been understood that human interaction is in large part comprised of scripts (Schank & Abelson, 1977). The more exposure to and experience we have with various scripts, the more able interactants we become. Television in many ways provides an opportunity for its viewers to enhance their repertoires of interpersonal verbal routines in that the television genre requires personalities on the screen to stick closely to a particular, well-thought-out script. Consequently, when interpersonal communication is portrayed via television, the result is dialog that is not only contextually embedded, but is composed with close forethought as to that important link of dialogue and the context in which it evolves. In some ways television dialog is the antithesis of foreign and second language instructional materials where context is often an afterthought with primary emphasis being on graded *linguistic content*.

Narratives are, by nature, also carefully scripted. Like reading, the more one views television, the larger becomes one's store of blueprints and narrative devices. The larger the store of narrative plans and devices experienced, the more readily one is able to comprehend additional stories by reconciling what is novel with what one already knows about the anatomy of narrative (Fisher, 1987; Fiske, 1987; Luke, 1985). Research on children and television finds strong parallels between the manner in which stories depicted through visual and aural media are processed and the ways in which children understand written stories (Kelly, 1981). Underlying these parallel processes is the notion about the schemata that viewers, like readers, bring to television processing and comprehension. The growth of text literacy skills is contingent on familiarity with textual and narrative conventions. The more one grows familiar with story "blueprints," the more facile the processing task and the deeper the level of understanding. The ease and depth of television comprehension is likewise dependent on a viewer's viewing history; that is, the size of an individual's repertoire of various visual, aural and narrative schemas (Collins, 1981). Children, for example, respond to known production conventions more as they grow older and as their experiences with television accumulate. Katz and Liebes (1986) reported that "Even children, who do not understand the meanings intended by the producer, understand something and shape what they think they are seeing in light of their experience with life and with the conventions of the medium" (p. 188). As such, it can be said that these blueprints for understanding what one views and reads are truly critical to successful comprehension. As with text, if one is unfamiliar with a television convention such as foreshadowing, key information needed to process the storyline is lost. In effect, therefore, as one watches more television, viewing literacy is enhanced and comprehension in turn increases.

Activating and employing preexisting schemata to make what is seen and heard meaningful is a fundamental comprehension strategy. Mass-media theorists conceptualize television along similar lines (Altheide & Snow, 1979). That is, "Audience members come to acquire a sophisticated series of expectations which they bring to their consumption of television" (Traudt & Lont, 1987, p. 161). Viewers employ these expectations when processing and decoding what they view, just as prior experiential knowledge comes into play when people make sense of what they hear and read. With few exceptions, human beings are television consumers and, therefore, possess such viewing schema and competencies. Life experiences in conjunction with viewing competencies would predict that television viewing is an activity which implies a level of comprehension on the part of viewers regardless of any unfamiliarity with the language and culture depicted. Persons with limited skills in that language and culture have at their disposal a repertoire of viewing literacy skills that can assist their decoding of novel aural input. There is evidence which indicates that schemata activated through aural and visual channels does in fact facilitate comprehension of complex linguistic input in a foreign or second language (Mueller, 1980).

VERBAL ABILITY: COMPLEMENTARY OR CONFLICTING INFLUENCE?

There is little doubt that an activity which takes up 3 to 6 hours of a child's day impacts beliefs, behavior, and cognitive processes. But how does extensive attention to a medium, that in addition to being highly visual is to a large degree verbal, impact viewers' verbal skills and competencies? Relatively little is understood in terms of television's effect on children's linguistic growth. On the one hand, it is arguable that the time spent viewing television is time taken away from other language and literacy activities that may be more meaningful; that is, interpersonal interaction (Fisher, 1984) and reading (Morgan & Gross, 1982; Selnow & Bettinghaus, 1982). Fisher (1984), for example, examined the argument that the quality of language experiences through television programming is limited. Limitations cited include sound distortion (as compared to real life speech), lack of clarity of nonverbal cuing as an aid to comprehension, and, due to a passive, one-way viewing structure, "the loss of initiating power" on the part of the child (p. 86). In developing her conflict model of television viewing and language development, Fisher contrasted television talk with motherese and pointed out television's deficiencies as a source of simplified input for children learning their first language.

Rice (1983, 1984) countered these proposed deficiencies by making the case that simplified aural input, although helpful, is not in fact a requirement for first language acquisition. She argued that television can be viewed as a powerful medium of models whose use of language is lively and highly contextualized and that these qualities motivate child viewers to process language deeply in order to understand what they watch.

Although the argument can be made that time spent viewing television is time not spent reading, there is also evidence that lower SES children, those whose range of experience is limited, derive benefits from television viewing as it expands their experiential base and gives them a sense of the composition of the larger world. This enlarged sense of the world and vicarious experiences within it can be viewed, therefore, as contributing to children's ability to understand and to read.

Additional first language studies that examine television's effect on verbal abilities focus on simultaneous visual and aural input as either complementary or conflicting. One study found that children less competent in language use experience television as competing modalities (aural and visual). Children consequently choose to attend to the visual at the expense of aural processing (Donaldson, 1976; Fisher, 1984). Contrary evidence emerges in the work of Peeck (1974) and Mueller (1980), who found that visual input in fact complements aural input and can aid comprehension rather than detract from it. Another first language study of television's effect on verbal growth finds a radical decrease in children's attention to the aural and an increase in attention to the visual as linguistic complexity increases (Hawkins, Yong-ho, & Pingree, 1991). However, with regard to television's effect on language skills overall, empirical results are limited. Assessment has been typically tied to reading ability as opposed to overall linguistic competence. Selnow and Bettinghaus (1982), for example, found negative inverse relationships between reading ability in the first language and amount of television exposure.

Research on television's influence on first language verbal ability presents conflicting evidence. On the one hand, there are indications that television viewing is a poor form of the kind of language input which enhances verbal abilities. In addition, there is some evidence that time spent watching television reduces time dedicated to other activities deemed more likely to enhance linguistic and sociolinguistic skills. On the other hand, some research suggests that television may complement first language acquisition processes. This research demonstrates that television is input-rich; that is, that programming consists of "minipackages of televised information that constitutes small lessons in the meanings and grammatical role of certain words" (Rice, 1983, p. 220). In sum, one set of studies indicates that television viewing is tied to weaker cognitive investment, whereas another set holds that television viewers actively process verbal meaning in conjunction with visually packed messages. The remainder of this chapter argues that proficiency in *second* language (L2) skills are uniquely enhanced by watching television because of the greater cognitive investment of the L2 learner in the act of viewing.

TV VIEWING AND SECOND LANGUAGE ACQUISITION

Several cases have been made for the use of videotape as a tool in second and foreign language instruction (MacWilliam, 1986; Meskill, 1991; Penfield, 1987; Secules, Herron & Tomasello, 1992; Stempleski & Tomalin, 1992; Tudor, 1987; Willis, 1983). Although it is commonly held that videotape can serve as a powerful tool for second language instruction, the role of television outside of the classroom and the link between these viewing practices and the classroom have not as yet been addressed.

There is a conflicting view of television and the growth of verbal abilities for second language learners as well. Snow et al. (1976), for example, reported no effect of television viewing on ESL learners' acquisition of English. Likewise, it has been speculated that for viewers watching television in their second language, linguistic complexity coupled with multiple processing modalities can derail efficient aural comprehension (Singer, 1980). On the other hand, contradictory evidence exists that points to increased fluency in bilinguals directly resulting from consistent viewing of Public Television shows such as *Sesame Street* and *Carrascolendas* (Williams & Natalicio, 1978). Either way, nonnative speakers of English in this country and abroad do watch television; it therefore can be inferred that the medium has something to offer besides aural dissonance. Watching television in a second or foreign language is demanding, yet we can assume it carries some reward for the viewer.

In an activity such as reading in a second language, L2 learners have a critical cognitive advantage in that they can control pacing and thereby afford themselves ample time to decode and reflect on the meaning of the texts they read. Television viewing, on the other hand, requires real-time decoding with little or no time for significant deciphering and reflection. Unless viewing prerecorded TV programming on a VCR, viewers cannot stop, slow down, or repeat the action if they do not understand. Moreover, viewing requires simultaneous processing of visual and aural data that must be rendered meaningful within contexts that may be only partially familiar to second language viewers.

In a rare inquiry into the effects of TV viewing on second language acquisition, Blosser (1988) conducted a study of Mexican and Puerto Rican children learning English as a second language in the United States. Of interest were the effects of television viewing on first and second language reading ability. The study revealed moderately positive correlations between time spent watching television and reading ability when viewing was limited to 3 hours per day. This finding held, however, only with students who had some English skills. Monolingual Spanish-speaking children, the author surmised, lacked sufficient skills to find television programming comprehensible and, therefore, their reading skills benefited little or not at all from their viewing time. Limited English Proficient (LEP) students with some English, on the other hand, appear to benefit from limited hours spent processing the second language input.

THE INQUIRY

Although the majority of adolescent LEP students struggle with English and with maintaining their age/grade level in English while in school, they are at the same time engaging in an out-of-school activity that requires relatively intensive work with the language with which they are otherwise at odds. In an attempt to begin to understand the nature of L2 television viewing and its possible influence on second language acquisition, the following questions are addressed:

- What television shows do adolescent Learners of English as a Second Language students prefer to watch?
- What is particularly compelling/motivating about the programs they prefer?
- What makes these programs distinctive in terms of content and comprehensibility?
- What are the implications of this viewing for linguistic development outside of the classroom and also within?

PROGRAMMING SELECTION

The literature on viewer programming selection points to four key features that determine what gets viewed on television: familial influence, peer influence, scheduling, and channel loyalty (Heeter & Greenberg, 1985). Program-specific influences have been identified as the presence of music, humor, and peer identification (Wakshlag, 1985). The latter factors are treated in the upcoming section on programming analysis.

One strong factor influencing which TV programs are watched is familial preferences in tandem with a household's communicative patterns that center on television viewing (Bryce, 1987; Wolf, Meyer, & White, 1982). It is clear that family setting impacts programming preferences in general. Interestingly, however, input from LEP siblings may exert more influence than parental input because siblings most often share dual language status and could therefore be expected to be more adept at modeling programming selection and at engaging in talk that is tied to what is viewed in the target language (R. Santiago, personal communication Sept. 1992). Additionally, Atkin (1985) pointed to four key motivators for viewing selection: *conversational material, advice, learning about life,* and *learning new behaviors.* The first motivator, conversational material, is an important factor for adolescents. To be part of the crowd, one must share experiences about which to converse. Television programming selection can also be influenced by additional socio- and psychological need. As such, programs may be selected based on the need for receiving advice and guidance in making day-to-day as well as larger life decisions. Learning about life and learning about behavior are also particularly salient motivators for this age group. Television offers a means of learning about what others do and about how society operates. Viewers can thus gain insight into others' thoughts, feelings, morals, and motivations to which they can compare and with which they can refine their own beliefs and actions. Among adolescents, therefore, preferences for television shows tend to develop from social contexts (Wolf, 1987) and evolve into program and even station loyalties. Viewing patterns can work to bond social group ties over the long term: the programs and characters favored by one's peers influence programming selection throughout childhood and adolescence (Gunter, 1985).

Regarding the influence of time, Heeter and Greenberg (1985) reported that program scheduling is the number one factor that determines what is viewed on television. As we see here later, programs cited as preferred by the second language learning adolescents surveyed tend to be scheduled in both after school and early prime time slots. This is in keeping with National Broadcasting surveys which indicate that after-school sitcom viewing is second only to Saturday-morning program viewing in terms of popularity among school-age children.

Beyond the influences of family, peers, and program scheduling lies what is for this inquiry a key issue: the issue of accessibility and comprehensibility. It is assumed that beyond these factors, the degree to which a program is understandable for a nonnative speaker influences both what is viewed and the level of viewing involvement. Analysis of the genre of programs most frequently viewed by learners of English as a second language provides a basis on which to judge the comprehensibility issue as a possible influence of viewing selection.

SURVEY DATA

Data on viewing preferences of learners of English as a second language was collected in two batches. One hundred and fifty-five junior and senior high English as a second language students made up the largest group of second language learning subjects. The second group consisted of 18 Yugoslav high school students learning English as a foreign language (EFL) on a summer exchange program.

Both groups were supplied a questionnaire to complete as part of a speaking/writing class activity. In each case, once having completed the questionnaire individually, participants were encouraged to share and discuss their preferences as a group. This was typically done by constructing and completing a matrix of class-viewing habits and drawing conclusions about group habits and preferences.

The majority of students in both the U.S. and Yugoslav groups reported watching television for between 1 and 3 hours per day (42.9%), with the smallest number viewing more than 7 hours per day (8.4%; see Figure 4.1).

How Many Hours Do You Watch Television Each Day?

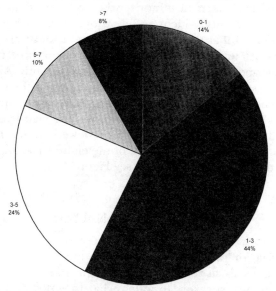

Figure 4.1. Number of hours spent viewing television

WHAT NNS DID *NOT* WATCH

It is interesting to note that although nonnative children and adults report learning English via children's programming on Public Broadcasting Service channels, not one of the individuals surveyed reported watching public television. Nor did they report viewing programs specifically designed for ESL learners.

Participants cited news broadcasts as the most difficult to comprehend and in not one case did students surveyed report watching the news on television or listening to radio news. When asked to comment on genres of programming subjects found the easiest to understand, there was consistency across the board in terms of both types and features of those shows they found eased comprehension and those that posed barriers to comprehension. These programming genres are:

Difficult	*Easy*
news	situation comedies
ethnic English	teen dramas
sports	MTV
movies	movies
mysteries	

Figure 4.2 represents the reported viewing preferences of the 173 subjects. Apart from a small minority who reported that they enjoyed watching sports and music videos on television, the overwhelming majority of subjects stated that their favorite television shows were family situation comedies. *Alf* was rated among individuals' top three favorites with *The Cosby Show* and *Growing Pains* running close seconds. Although data on high school students viewing U.S. programming in their native countries was limited to eighteen interviews, results regarding programming preferences closely parallel those of second language learners in this country. That is, of eighteen students interviewed, fifteen reported *The Cosby Show* as their favorite with twelve of the eighteen stating that *Alf* was their among their top three favorites (see Figure 4.2).

PROGRAMMING ANALYSIS

Beyond criteria for programming selection investigated in the studies cited earlier, there exists relatively little information that pertains to what motivates nonnative speakers to watch what they do. This discussion is concerned with that motivation in light of comprehensibility for viewers whose competence in English is otherwise challenged by the target language environment and with the resulting language acquisition potential of, what will be argued, is an important language acquisition activity.

The following programming analysis focuses on (a) possible attributes of preferred programming that render these more linguistically accessible for nonnative speakers; and (b) implications that these programming preferences and the characteristics of preferred programs carry for L2 acquisition. In other words, the structural features of preferred programs are analyzed with a view toward understanding how their features render complex interpersonal interaction accessible for nonnative speakers.

In this case, family situation comedies (sitcoms) were reported as the overwhelming favorite for the adolescents surveyed. What attributes of sitcoms may be rendering these shows linguistically accessible? Production quality, characters, and contexts of the sitcom genre are analyzed. A detailed analysis of the popular sitcom *Alf* provides a specific secondary level of analysis.

Production Quality

The production quality of film—lighting, camera movement, and special effects—is unique to that artform. When we watch film, we are required

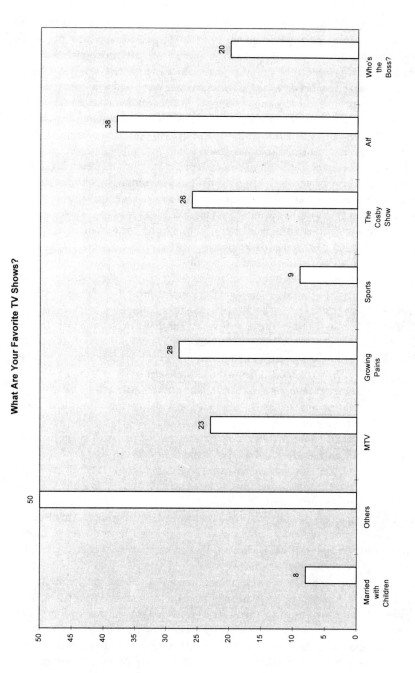

Figure 4.2. Programs preferred by participants

to assemble images in order to make sense of setting, plot, and characters, inferring meaning from what we see and what people say and do. The more elaborate the production quality, therefore, the more demanding viewer processing becomes and the less control we as viewers can exert over the experience (Fiske, 1987). Sitcoms are very low on the scale of required interpretive processing. Whereas film is textured and evocative, sitcoms are flat and representational. One's level of involvement, therefore, is less connected to what titillates the eye and intellect and more in tune to what gets said and what gets done.

With the exception of the occasional bedroom or exterior shot, sitcom sets are comprised of living rooms and kitchens. These remain the same living rooms and kitchens from week to week. Lighting changes are limited to day versus night, interior versus exterior. It is the sameness of these familiar sets that (a) gives the sitcom genre "much of its charm" (Jones, 1992, p. 6) and (b) aids in placing more emphasis on dialog and interpersonal activity than on setting. Scenes, moreover, are typically static within these spaces. When combined with camera movement and switching/editing that focuses on interpersonal interaction, what gets said and done within these spaces becomes very straightforward. Although this kind of staging may at first blush appear to render the drama bland, it is in fact these characteristics that potentially enhance aural and visual comprehension in that emphasis is not on the environment, but on the human interaction within it. The mind is consequently drawn to action and highly directed *interaction*. As such, the genre pulls attention toward character demeanor and to what, how and why things get communicated both verbally and nonverbally.

In terms of camera shots, a large amount of physical space is typically left around each individual as she or he is delivering lines. While aiding the viewer with explicit visual information regarding location, the long shot also aids in defining characters' ethos and intentions, as we can see a good deal of the environment in which and with which the character is interacting (e.g., the people on whom what is said produces an effect). Visual space is most typically concentrated on dyads: the majority of interaction is between pairs of individuals with the camera aimed at capturing the dynamics of these two-way conversations. Camera shots focus on the reactions of interlocutors. Close-ups are limited to these reaction shots; that is, one conversation participant responding to what the other is saying and doing. Spatial orientation through long shots as well as explicit shots of interlocutors' reactions are powerful cues for comprehension of what is being communicated between characters. Meringoff et al. (1983) found evidence that television viewers make continual use of such production qualities to formulate inferences regarding the meanings and storyline of a show. When comprehension is limited by facility with the English language, such characteristics become critical aids to understanding.

Another production characteristic of the sitcom that facilitates comprehension is live studio or "canned" (prerecorded) laughter. Sitcom characters' discourse is punctuated by titters and guffaws, hoots and groans from the audience. These signals provide the viewer key information regarding interactional turns and the meanings behind what is said and done. They cue viewers to instances where what is said and what is done are partitioned and mark the distribution and rhythms of both verbal and nonverbal events. These aural signals, in other words, mark points at which a turn has been completed and let viewers know when something amusing and/or shocking has just occurred. In addition to audience cues, music is also used in sitcoms to denote shifts in mood and changes in scenes. These aural cues serve as signals for viewers as to the meanings of conversation, action and storyline. In terms of aural comprehensibility, sitcoms are, moreover, the TV genre of exaggerated speech. Speech is slow and overenunciated in order for everyone to "get the joke." In addition to clear speech, there is also a quantity of enlarged nonverbal accompaniment (exaggerated gestures) to what is being said.

Straightforward visual treatment, specific camera angles, exaggerated speech, and paralinguistic cues, coupled with audience and musical punctuation, can be viewed as rendering what gets said and done in sitcoms more easily comprehensible. For nonnative speakers, the presence and emphasis of only those features most essential to comprehension also lowers affect and thereby renders the sitcom viewing experience a relaxed one. As such, language learners are more apt to successfully process aural and visual input (Dulay, Burt & Krashen, 1982; Tudor, 1987).

In review, therefore, the following production qualities potentially assist viewer comprehension and may be drawing learners of English as a second language to the family sitcom genre:

- static, familiar sets
- limited inference required by staging
- full-figure shots
- reaction shots
- focus on dyads
- paralinguistic cues
- audience/musical punctuation
- exaggerated speech

Characters

Even though situation comedies are typically classified as *never-realism* (Dworetzky, 1992), their characters, however fictional, nonetheless represent communicative behaviors and strategies that *work*, albeit in a fictionalized and often fantastic context. An almost intimate familiarity with characters' lives, trials, motives, and personalities develops rapidly with repeated viewing. Once viewers become familiar with and, in turn, involved with characters, speech and actions take on a predictability that renders what is said and done more readily comprehensible. Therefore, these fictional beings can be considered powerful models of communication skills and strategies: What they accomplish with words and gestures is most often made explicit through clear, visual consequences.

Overtly perfect, rotten, or naive characters can lend an almost transcendental sense to the viewing process. They are at once identifiable and real in that through their speech and actions they effect immediately perceptible changes in their environments, and unreal by virtue of caricature. In terms of modeling how matters get communicated in English, the "caricaturish" nature of sitcom personalities, coupled with their exaggerated enunciation and intonation, also make them considerably powerful sociolinguistic models. Second language theory and research, moreover, affirms that models of the target language and culture that represent students' in-group are considered superior to out-of-group models (Dulay et al., 1982). Second language learners are therefore more apt to attend to and thus learn from in-group models of the target language. In an ethnographic study with native speaker children, Wolf (1987), for example, found that children consistently prefer that with which they can most closely identify. Children of all cultures find their role models and methods of organizing their feelings through fictional TV characters. It is important to note that sitcoms identified as favorites among these LEP populations are peopled by nuclear families complete with children with whom this age group can identify.

Context

The action and humor in family sitcoms center on personal problems and the trials of daily life. When considering experiences LEP students bring to television, those with which they are most intimately familiar are most likely families and the ethos of family life. As such, characters along with their feelings and concerns match blueprints these viewers use to decode the interpersonal workings of family and its daily challenges. Within the family context are universal themes such as relationships, feelings, winning and losing, tensions between family members, and so on. It seems highly probable that LEP students can therefore readily identify with what goes on in this broadcast genre.

In addition to the power of identification with characters as it factors in to comprehensibility is another aspect that is not the sole domain of family sitcoms, but which is prevalent in all representational drama.

This is what I will call *The Dallas Factor*. In watching or reading a story about fictional people, as human beings our interest and motivation are piqued when what we read about or see is intrinsically stimulating. Edgar Allen Poe characterized this human trait as the "perverse imp" in all humans: the naughty djinn that drives us to find pleasure in that which is sublime because it is off limits. We are, in short, motivated by intrigue and scandal. When presented with a window through which we can observe others saying and doing those things we either consciously or subliminally abhor and/or yearn to do ourselves, a perverse satisfaction results. In the past decade, television has become most satisfying in this respect. What distinguishes sitcoms over other genres of television narratives is that it provides dual forms of satisfaction: the perverse imp gets satisfaction due to the voyeurism aspect, *and* sitcoms consistently provide satisfying resolution to everyday problems.

Sitcoms seem to fit the narrative blueprints and competencies that these adolescents are in the midst of developing. Their humorous treatment of the taboo and profane in turn satisfy voyeur desires. Students can peer into a window at a slice of U.S. life that intrigues by virtue of ready identification with aspects of characters and context. Intrigue, moreover, is present through the marginal and/or zany. In short, sitcoms are comprehensible because they are both satisfying and captivating.

ALF

Alf, the long-running situation comedy (1986-1990), was elected an almost unanimous favorite by groups of both ESL and EFL learners. The show continues to be rerun on cable television and, like other popular sitcom staples, is typically broadcast during afterschool scheduling slots. Abroad, rebroadcasts of the show are still aired during primetime. The main character, Alf, an acronym for Alien Life Form, is an odd-looking, yet somehow cuddly being from a distant planet who ends up a permanent house guest of a middle-class nuclear U.S. family.

Alf is the embodiment of those family sitcom attributes previously discussed. Production quality, characters, and context are entirely in keeping with the genre as a whole. With the exception of comic flashbacks and dream sequences, the overall context, sets, and characters remain the same episode after episode. Scenes are relatively static with lighting changes limited to day versus night effects. Camerawork is also limited to establishing and reaction shots. Alf and the members of his adopted family speak slowly. Their verbal delivery is so deliberate that it almost seems they are speaking to a nonnative audience. The overall effect of this purposeful speaking style is that there is ample time within conversations to process and in turn "get" double entendres, plays on words and the recurring joke.

Jokes and puns are delivered in short, simple sentences. Reactions are marked by interlocutor facial expressions and by the program's laugh-track. Characters overenunciate as if they believed they were being observed by Alf's alien cohorts back on Malmack.

A characteristic that distinguishes *Alf* is its overarching theme of alienation. An alien from a distant planet finds himself immersed in U.S. culture and is forced by his uniqueness to maintain a marginal, albeit amusing role while taking refuge in the home of his host family. His appearance is bizarre, his home culture radically different. Rather than capitalize on these differences negatively, Alf's character is cast in a positive light that underscores the value of being different in the U.S. Although there are those who do not know and understand Alf for who he truly is and, if they did, would predictably exploit his "otherness" for sensation and personal gain, those who know him love and accept him for who he is beyond the radical differences between his being and their own. This theme of accepting differences reflects "the new domestic coalition" the United States is forging. Television reinforces the trend by communicating that "from our modern alienation, weirdness, and hostility will come a happy family" (Jones, 1992, p. 262).

At a certain level, Alf's situation can be seen as analogous to the forced immersion situation of many children of immigrants and refugees. Finding oneself in a foreign environment, one must cope with that which is in conflict with one's own basic beliefs and understandings of the world. In Alf's case, the character possesses a world view that helps him to render the "alien" situation manageable through a supportive social network and humor. As he sorts out U.S. culture's idiosyncracies, he pokes fun. Alf's humor is frequently manifest in visual jokes: he likes to dress up in human clothing and accessories and busies himself by finding unique uses for household objects and fiddles with absurd gadgets.

The viewer is privy to Alf's past life and fantasy life through flash-back and dream sequences that allow us to (a) share his current world view by becoming familiar with his personal history (b) come to see his inner thoughts and feelings beyond his humorous antics. Alf is not the least reticent to share and express his feelings with his human family. The theme of alienation is ever present in these revelations. He's different. He can't fit in. The family hides him from being discovered by outsiders. They protect him. He understands this but yearns to "go public" and be a part of the American scene about which he loves to joke. In this exchange, Willy, father of the nuclear family, enters the kitchen as Alf is typing:

> *Willy:* I assume this is more than typing practice.
> *Alf:* It's my press release. I've decided to reveal myself to the world. That way I can meet new people, travel, see a Grateful Dead concert . . . [laughtrack]

Willy: Alf, I don't think the authorities would even let you go out in public let alone become a Dead Head. [laughtrack] You'd become government property.
Alf: That's fine. As long as I've got my freedom.

Later in the show, Alf is convinced by his family and friends that revealing himself to the world would be disastrous. During a surprise party in his honor (he had become depressed due to the cancellation of the press conference he had been looking forward to and is given a special party to cheer him up), his support network is reinforced. At the surprise party, Carol, the mother speaks:

Carol: Alf, we wanted to show you that your world wasn't as limited as you thought. We know it's not the same as going out and making new friends, but we hope it helps.
Alf: I couldn't ask for more. [aw . . . from audience] [long pause, exchange of meaningful looks] Now where's the presents! [laughtrack]

Beyond the program's apparent comprehensibility, which is representative of the genre as a whole, themes and the plight of the show's star may be an attraction for nonnative viewers. As Altheide and Snow (1979) pointed out, "The audience member is selectively attentive to particular kinds of media and media content for the purpose of validating personal identifiers" (cited in Traudt & Lont, 1987, p. 142).

SUMMARY

Programming favored by LEP adolescents apparently resonates and entertains to the extent that these viewers will work at comprehending the language with which they struggle during the school day. From the preceding analysis of the preferred genre of television shows, it can be concluded that this type of program offers those with limited skills in comprehending English particular production qualities that render it comprehensible as well as themes to which they can relate their experiences. These two facts in tandem—that children apparently are motivated to view these television shows and that they consequently work at comprehending this kind of seminaturalistic linguistic input—cast television viewing in the role of providing an important form of practice in one of the most daunting aspects of learning a foreign language: comprehension of aural input and an inside view of sociolinguistic and socioculture "norms" of the host country.

IMPLICATIONS

Although the long periods of time these LEP students appear to spend processing target language input would predict growth in linguistic skills, whether this viewing positively impacts overall language competency remains to be determined through extensive empirical research. It is arguable, however, that based on its characteristics of comprehensibility, this out-of-school viewing carries strong implications for language acquisition and cultural assimilation.

It has already been pointed out that LEP viewers, like all viewers, are likely to possess some level of television viewing literacy. That is, through their experiences watching TV in their own and in the host culture, they have attained a level of proficiency in interpreting visual information as it corresponds to the aural. It is through exposure to the medium that this form of literacy grows and strengthens, just as more reading increases text literacy (Fiske, 1987). What the family sitcom genre offers LEP children is straightforward implementation of the proficiencies they have gained from media and real world experiences: they are familiar with this form of narrative and can therefore lay the templates they have cultivated within their native cultures on top of U.S. versions (Katz & Liebes, 1986). Their most immediate experiential store—the practices and nuances of family life—constitute experiences that they can again transpose on the televised version of life in the host culture. Processing what goes on in half an hour dense with target language and cultural information is consequently facilitated by virtue of the medium in general and the characteristics of the family sitcom in particular.

Unlike earlier arguments that second language learners might be learning language through television by mimicry (Asante, 1982)—an argument induced by outdated perceptions of the language acquisition process—current theory in the field of Second Language Acquisition argues that television represents a source of comprehensible input (Garza, 1991; MacWilliam, 1986; Tudor, 1987; Vanderplank, 1988). The term *comprehensible input* refers to the ideal type of verbal materials that is critical for second and foreign language learners to encounter and cognitively process in order to acquire the target language. The match between the criteria of comprehensible input and output attributes of the U.S. family sitcom is tight:

- ingroup models of the target language in use are superior
- input must be relevant to students' lives; motivating
- input must be authentic/representative of meaningful communication
- input must be at a slightly higher level of difficulty than the student's current level of competence

- input should be encountered in mass quantities (Dulay et al., 1982)

In addition to these characteristics for comprehensible input is an additional feature of second language acquisition that is supported by television viewing; that which is known as the Silent Period (Krashen & Terrell, 1983). When acquiring a new language, it is argued, it is imperative that before attempting to speak we come in contact with a great deal of aural input so as to acquire a feel for and familiarity with the contours of the target language, its noises, and tonal nuances. Television as a backdrop to many home activities might also be considered a source of information regarding the rhythms, cadence, and sound system of the new language. It is through an initial familiarity with these aspects of the language that one can come to master comprehending and then finally producing it.

As we have seen from the analysis of the sitcom genre, desirable characteristics of target language input with which the LEP child needs to come in contact in order for successful acquisition to take place are in fact characteristics of the kinds of television shows that LEP children are likely to spend their leisure time viewing. The question remains as to how an activity that appears to be providing optimal aural processing of the target language outside of schools (whose goal is to provide support to students in these very same processes) can inform actual attitudes and practices.

Learning to mean in a second language is clearly a social process best mitigated by appropriate second language curricula in conjunction with naturalistic contact with the target language and culture. However, as clearly accessible models of native speaker discourse practices in which second language learners need to engage for significant periods of time, television sitcoms can be considered a powerful socializing agent for LEP adolescents. Children are spending a significant portion of their day processing aural and visual input in the language with which they otherwise struggle in the academic environment. Schools need to acknowledge and value these out-of-school activities and build bridges between the two worlds that, without television, may otherwise be absent.

Making connections between those aspects of the host culture with which LEP children have cultivated a certain familiarity through watching television and the social and linguistic demands of the academic context is a potential facilitative role of school personnel. Television viewing can serve as much-needed common ground for native speaker peers and teachers. Oftentimes the latter, being unfamiliar with the LEP child's language and culture, are at a loss to find this common ground on which to build conversation and solidarity. Insights, then, into what LEP children do outside of the school day can facilitate in-school communication. When the activity is television, shared knowledge and experience can help bond otherwise culturally divergent groups. Moreover, the very topic of television shows familiar to students represents a powerful catalyst for communication that can serve not only to stimulate interpersonal interaction around what is meaningful to children, but establish and maintain much-needed coherence between what goes on at home and in the classroom.

An inherent quality of television viewing is that it promotes talk between viewers (Katz & Liebes, 1986; Lynch, 1985; Morley, 1986). Shared viewing stimulates an enormous amount of real and varied discourse that, due to the high degree of relevancy to everyday, contemporary American experience, pertains directly to the lives and opinions of conversation participants (Traudt & Lont, 1987). As a springboard for discussions and activities centered on U.S. culture and on how family life is similar and/or different from students' home cultures, sitcoms not only serve as a rich source of talk, but also link thoughts and feelings expressed to common outside of class viewing experiences. Talking about television shows is an activity in which children naturally engage. It is a socializing activity and, as such, a source of solidarity and group identification—something that ethnically marginalized children are in need of more than anyone. Moreover, the variation of linguistic requirements for such communication is vast. Talking about television as a means of linguistic and cultural development, therefore, offers a wide range of speech act possibilities on the part of students (Spanos & Smith, 1990).

LEP adolescents are faced with the challenge of adapting to and developing personal identity within dual cultures. Like their native counterparts, these children are logically using television to develop their identities and are comparing how experiences get managed in their world with how fictionalized in-group characters manage their experiences. For both native and nonnative speakers of English, television represents a window on the social experiences of others with which to compare their own beliefs and behaviors (Fenigstein & Heyduk, 1985). It is a means for satisfying curiosity about the private behaviors of others—an opportunity that is otherwise limited to direct experience. Television viewing, moreover, plays a role in the maintenance of personal self; that is, in how we carry out and participate in social interactions. As such, television can be seen as providing to LEP children models of how meaning gets negotiated within the target culture and how things get done in English.

Exposure to rich English language input via TV is constant for these youngsters. How can this activity be capitalized on? Some ESL learners who are "good at language" may develop or already have strategies to exercise in making sense of what they hear and see; others may become as frustrated with media input as they are with their attempts in general to learn the language. For these kinds of learners, guided development in media literacy—how to listen and view—is a valuable exercise for an

English as a second language or mainstream instructor to provide. Salomon (1983), for example, has found that focused viewing, as opposed to mindless viewing, results in increased learning from television. Likewise, at least one research effort with language learners has demonstrated the effectiveness of previewing and focused viewing tasks as means of improving target language comprehension (Garza, 1991). Another collected self-reports from ESL learners who watched television in the target language; these reports reveal that individuals do develop more and more efficient strategies for dealing with multimodal linguistic input as the amount of viewing increases (Vanderplank, 1988).

In-school viewing literacy activities can potentially augment the amount of benefit that results from LEP student's out-of-school viewing. The more actively involved these children are in their viewing activities, the more gains in linguistic and cultural understanding we might expect them to achieve. Bryce (1987) pointed out that, "An active audience brings to the reception a personal competence in television use which has been developed and negotiated in daily interaction, most often in family settings" (p. 121). Development and negotiation of these competencies can fruitfully be extended into the arena of the classroom, where television can play a critical socializing role by establishing a common ground between and among peers and mentors. LEP children can in turn pass viewing literacy skills and strategies on to their parents (who may be struggling with English as well) and, in doing so, can encourage social family viewing practices deemed beneficial for linguistic and cultural growth among native speakers (Spigel, 1992; Traudt & Lont, 1987).

CONCLUSION

Beyond television, sociolinguistic models of the English language in use and the U.S. culture in action are in most cases limited for language minority children. This is true of the adolescents surveyed in this study whose nationalities are represented by fairly large minicommunities and cultural enclaves where people are in more frequent contact with speakers of their native language. Even children born in the United States as offspring of first-generation immigrants—children whose families do not provide models of the target language and culture—are greater than average TV consumers. This more frequent consumption compensates for input otherwise not readily available in the home (Iiyama & Kitano, 1982; Lampkin, 1976).

There is clearly a myriad of intertwined and complex variables associated with the effects of television viewing on the socialization of children. As regards the linguistic and sociolinguistic development of language minority adolescents, exposure to clear, accessible, and motivating models of the English language in use as well as the cognitive growth implied from extended periods of aural processing make television in general, and family situation comedies in particular, powerful influences that ought not be understated. Television represents a private window into U.S. culture otherwise not readily observable to nonnative speakers of English. Scenes inside this window are linguistically, paralinguistically, and culturally rich. The sitcom *Alf,* identified as a favorite among both ESL and EFL learners, seems to additionally have themes and characters with which such viewers can identify or which they can at least appreciate as fantasy. One can only wonder what life in the host environment would be like without access to these comprehensible microworlds that nonnative speakers can observe, study, and use as building blocks in their language acquisition and acculturation processes.

This discussion was built on findings concerning LEP student viewing habits and preferences. Implications drawn from the findings are inferential and speculative and leave open key questions: Is linguistic and cultural growth a byproduct of viewing? How does this viewing time impact not only the development of English language skills but contribute to conceptualizations regarding the host culture? Given the extensive aural comprehension practice LEP students receive from TV viewing outside the classroom, careful empirical studies of their responses to television in terms of language skills acquired are needed. Clearly, careful empirical examination of LEP students' responses to television in terms of language and skills acquired given the extensive aural comprehension practice they receive outside the classroom would be welcomed.

REFERENCES

Altheide, D.L., & Snow, R.P. (1979). *Media logic.* Beverly Hills, CA: Sage.

Asante, M. (1982). Television and the language socialization of black children. In G. Berry & C. Mitchell-Kernan (Eds.), *Television and the socialization of the minority child* (pp. 135-149). New York: Academic Press.

Atkin, C. (1985). Informational utility and selective exposure to entertainment media. In D. Zillmann & J. Bryant (Eds.), *Selective exposure to communication* (pp. 63-91). Hillsdale, NJ: Erlbaum.

Blosser, B. (1988, Fall). Television, reading and oral language development: The case of the Hispanic child. *NABE Journal,* 21-42.

Bryce, J. (1987). Family time and television use. In T. Lindlof (Ed.), *Natural audiences* (pp. 121-138). Norwood, NJ: Ablex.

Coates, B., Pusser, E., & Goodman, I. (1976). The influence of *Sesame Street* and *Mister Roger's Neighborhood* on children's social behavior in the preschool. *Child Development, 47,* 138-144.

Collins, W. (1981). Schemata for understanding television. In H. Kelly & H. Gardner (Eds.), *Viewing children through television* (pp. 31-41). San Francisco, CA: Jossey-Bass.

Donaldson, M. (1976). *Children's minds.* London: Fontana.

Dulay, H., Burt, M., & Krashen, S. (1982). *Language two.* New York: Oxford University Press.

Dworetzky, T. (1992, April). Teens: Will TV become their virtual (and only) reality? *Omni Magazine.*

Fenigstein, A., & Heyduk, R. (1985). Thoughts and action as determinants of media exposure. In D. Zillmann & J. Bryant (Eds.), *Selective exposure to communication* (pp. 113-139). Hillsdale, NJ: Erlbaum.

Fisher, W. (1987). *Human communication as narration: Toward a philosophy of reason, value and action.* Columbia: University of South Carolina Press.

Fiske, J. (1987). *Television culture.* New York: Routledge.

Friedrich, L.K., & Stein, A.H. (1973). Aggressive and prosocial television programs and natural behavior in preschool children. *Monographs of the Society for Research in Child Development, 38*(3, No 151).

Garza, T. (1991). Evaluating the use of captioned video materials in advanced foreign language learning. *Foreign Language Annals, 2*(3), 239-258.

Gerbner, G., & Gross, L. (1976). Living with television: The violence profile. *Journal of Communication, 26*(2), 173-199.

Gunter, B. (1985). Determinants of television viewing preferences. In D. Zillmann & J. Bryant (Eds.), *Selective exposure to communication* (pp. 93-112). Hillsdale, NJ: Erlbaum.

Hawkins, R., Yong-ho, K., & Pingree, S. (1991). The ups and downs of attention to television. *Communication Research, 18*(1), 53-76.

Heeter, C., & Greenberg, B. (1985). Cable and program choice. In D. Zillmann & J. Bryant (Eds.), *Selective exposure to communication* (pp. 203-224.) Hillsdale, NJ: Erlbaum.

Iiyama, P., & Kitano, H. (1982). Asian Americans and the media. In G. Berry & C. Mitchell-Kernan (Eds.), *Television and the socialization of the minority child* (pp. 151-186) New York: Academic Press.

Jones, G. (1992). *Honey, I'm home! Sitcoms: Selling the American dream.* New York: Grove Weidenfeld.

Katz, E., & Liebes, T. (1986). Mutual aid in the decoding of Dallas: Preliminary notes from a cross-cultural study. In P. Drummond & R. Paterson (Eds.), *Television in transition* (pp. 187-198). London: British Film Institute.

Kelly, H. (1981). Reasoning about realities: Children's evaluations of television and books. In H. Kelly & H. Gardner (Eds.), *Viewing children through television* (pp. 59-71). San Francisco: Jossey-Bass.

Krashen, S., & Terrell, T. (1983). *The natural approach: Language acquisition in the classroom.* Oxford: Pergamon.

Lampkin, E. (1976). *Adolescent television use as a possible socialization agent: A cross-cultural comparison.* Unpublished doctoral dissertation, Stanford University, Stanford, CA.

Luke, C. (1985). Television discourse processing: A schema theoretic approach. *Communication Education, 34,* 91-105.

Lynch, A. (1985). The "unreality principle": One use of television commercials. *English Language Teaching Journal, 39*(2), 115-120.

MacWilliam, I. (1986). Video and language comprehension. *ELT Journal, 40*(2), 131-135.

Meringoff, L., Vibbert, M., Char, C., Fernie, D., Banker, G., & Gardner, H. (1983). How is children's learning from television distinctive? Exploiting the medium methodologically. In J. Bryant & D. Anderson (Eds.), *Children's understanding of television: Research on attention and comprehension* (pp. 151-177) New York: Academic Press.

Meskill, C. (1991). Multimedia and language learning: Assessing goals and system attributes. *CAELL Journal, 2*(2), 11-14.

Morgan, M., & Gross, L. (1982). Television and educational achievement and aspirations. In D. Pearl, L. Bouthilet, & J. Lazar (Eds.), *Television and behavior: Ten years of scientific progress and implications for the eighties* (pp. 78-90). Washington, DC: U.S. Government Printing Office.

Morley, D. (1986). *Family television: Cultural power and domestic leisure.* London: Comedia.

Mueller, G. (1980). Visual contextual cues and listening comprehension: An experiment. *Modern Language Journal, 64*(3), 335-340.

O'Connor, R. (1972). Modification of social withdrawal through symbolic modeling. In K. D. O'Leary & S. G. O'Leary (Eds.), *Classroom management* (pp. 235-248) New York: Pergamon.

Peeck, J. (1974). Retention of pictorial and verbal content of a text with illustrations, *Journal of Educational Psychology, 66,* 880-888.

Penfield, J. (1987). *The media: Catalysts for communicative language learning.* Reading, MA: Addison-Wesley.

Rice, M. (1983). The role of television in language acquisition. *Developmental Review, 3,* 211-224.

Rice, M. (1984). The words of children's television. *Journal of Broadcasting, 28*(4), 445-461.

Salomon, G. (1983). Television watching and mental effort: A social psychological view. In J. Bryant & D. Anderson (Eds.), *Children's understanding of television: Research on attention and comprehension* (pp. 181-196) New York: Academic Press.

Schank, R., & Abelson, R. (1977). *Scripts, plans, goals and understanding.* Hillsdale, NJ: Erlbaum.

Secules, T., Herron C., & Tomasello, M. (1992). The effect of video context on foreign language learning. *Modern Language Journal, 76*(4), 480-490.

Selnow, G., & Bettinghaus, E. (1982). Television exposure and language development. *Journal of Broadcasting, 26*(1), 469-479.

Singer, J. (1980). The power and limitations of television: A cognitive-affective analysis. In P. Annenbaum (Ed.), *The entertainment functions of television* (pp. 31-65). Hillsdale,. NJ: Erlbaum.

Snow, C., Arlmann-Rupp, A., Hassing, Y., Jobse, J., Joosten, J., & Vorster, J. (1976). Mothers' speech in three social classes. *Journal of Psycholinguistic Research, 5*, 1-20.

Spanos, G., & Smith, J. (1990). *Closed captioned television for adult LEP literacy learners.* (Eric Documentation Reproduction Service No. EDO-LE-90-04)

Spigel, L. (1992). *Make room for TV: Television and the family ideal in postwar America.* Chicago: University of Chicago Press.

Stempleski, S., & Tomalin, B. (1992). *Video in action: Recipes for using video in the language classroom.* Englewood Cliffs, NJ: Prentice-Hall.

Traudt, P., & Lont, C. (1987). Media-logic-in-use: The family as locus of study. In T. Lindlof (Ed.), *Natural audiences* (pp. 139-160). Norwood, NJ: Ablex.

Tudor, I. (1987). Video as a means of cultural familiarization. *System, 15*(2), 203-207.

Vanderplank, R. (1988). The value of teletext subtitles in language learning. *English Language Teaching Journal, 42*(4), 272-281.

Wakshlag, J. (1985). Selective exposure to educational television. In D. Zillmann & J. Bryant (Eds.), *Selective exposure to communication* (pp. 191-201). Hillsdale, NJ: Erlbaum.

Weekly Reader National Survey on Citizenship (1992, Spring). Middletown, CT: Weekly Reader Corporation.

Williams, F., & Natalicio, D. (1978). Evaluating *Carrascolendas:* A television series for Mexican American children. *Journal of Broadcasting, 16*, 299-307.

Willis, J. (1983). The role of the visual element in spoken discourse: Implications for the exploitation of video in the EFL classroom. In J. McGovern (Ed.), *Video applications in English language teaching* (pp. 29-42). New York: Pergamon Press.

Wolf, M. (1987). How children negotiate television. In T. Lindlof (Ed.), *Natural audiences* (pp. 58-94). Norwood, NJ: Ablex.

Wolf, M., Meyer, T., & White, C. (1982). A rule-based study of television's role in the construction of social reality. *Journal of Broadcasting, 26*(4), 813-829.

5

Social Learning from Saturday Morning Cartoons

Karen Swan
University at Albany

In 1982, the National Institute of Mental Health issued a report entitled *Television and Behavior*, which reviewed the over 2,500 available studies on television viewing and its effects on human development and behavior. Among many other issues, the report looked at the influences of television on attitudes, values, and beliefs, and found substantial evidence that people's attitudes and behaviors concerning violence, race, gender, sexuality, consumerism, and many other things could be significantly influenced by how much and what they watched on television. Its authors also concluded that television had become a major socializing agent of American children.

The report went on to state:

> In addition to socialization, television influences how people think about the world around them or what is sometimes called their conceptions of "social reality." Studies have been carried out on the amount of fear and mistrust of other people, and on the prevalence of violence, sexism, family values, racial attitudes, illness in the population, criminal justice, and affluence. On the whole, it seems that television leads its viewers to have television influenced attitudes. (p. 7)

In other words, viewers tend to accept and internalize the attitudes, values, and behaviors portrayed on broadcast television. No viewers are as vulnerable to such process as children.

Television provides all people with a window on the larger world, but the view through that window has a far greater influence on children's sense of it, simply because their individual worlds are so constricted, their experience so limited, and their perception of social reality so plastic. As

Dorr (1986) pointed out, the most important social learning usually occurs during childhood. "This is the time," she wrote, "when individuals learn what must be known if they are to function in their culture." (p. 13). When one considers that by the time they graduate from high school, American children will have spent more time in front of TV sets than in classrooms, it is not surprising that Dorr found that the major role broadcast television plays in children's lives is that of "an information providing experience—a source of knowledge or prejudice, a teacher of . . . how to play, fight, and love" (pg. 60).

Television depictions of social reality tend mainly to reinforce adults' world views. Children, on the other hand, especially young children, don't have preconceived notions about society and its workings, nor experience against which to test televised versions of these. They also, to a greater or lesser extent, tend to think everything they see on television is "real" (Christenson & Roberts, 1983). Indeed, our own research with 8- and 9-year-olds suggests they find the characters, situations, and story lines depicted even in Saturday morning cartoons realistic (Beasich, Leinoff, & Swan, 1992). In addition, children are more likely to be able to follow cartoon stories than those of other programs, hence, they are more likely to internalize the social realities depicted in them.

Saturday morning is the only block of programming time devoted exclusively to children. If television has become a major socializing agent of American children, then Saturday morning cartoons represent at least one of the primary texts for their social learning. This chapter examines that text through content and critical analyses of all programs broadcast between 8:00 a.m.. and 11:00 a.m. on Saturday, September 15, 1990, and again on Saturday, June 9, 1992 (after the Children's Television Act of 1990 went into effect). These included:

SEPTEMBER 15, 1990
Muppet Babies, 8–9 a.m., CBS
Garfield and Friends; 9–10 a.m., CBS
Teenage Mutant Ninja Turtles; 10–11 a.m., CBS
New Adventures of Winnie the Pooh; 8–8:30 a.m., ABC
The Wizard of Oz, 8:30–9 a.m., ABC
Slimer and the Real Ghostbusters; 9–10 a.m., ABC
Beetlejuice, 10–10:30 a.m., ABC
New Kids on the Block; 10:30–11 a.m., ABC
Camp Candy; 8–8:30 a.m., NBC
Captain N and Super Mario Brothers; 8:30–9:30 a.m., NBC
Gravedale High; 9:30–10 a.m., NBC
Kid N' Play; 10–10:30 a.m., NBC
The Chipmunks Go to the Movies; 10:30–11 a.m., NBC

JUNE 9, 1992

Captain Planet and the Planeteers; 8–9 a.m., CBS
Garfield and Friends; 9–10 a.m., CBS
Teenage Mutant Ninja Turtles; 10–11 a.m., CBS
New Adventures of Winnie the Pooh; 8–8:30 a.m., ABC
Land of the Lost; 8:30–9 a.m., ABC
Darkwing Duck; 9–9:30 a.m., ABC
Beetlejuice; 9:30–10:30 a.m., ABC
Slimer and the Real Ghostbusters; 10:30–11:30 a.m., ABC
Space Cats; 8–8:30 a.m., NBC
Yo, Yogi; 8:30–9 a.m., NBC
Captain N and Super Mario Brothers; 9–9:30 a.m., NBC
Pro Stars; 9:30–10 a.m., NBC
Wish Kid; 10–10:30 a.m., NBC
Saved By the Bell; 10:30–11 a.m., NBC

In reviewing the social reality depicted in Saturday morning cartoons, it is important to note that it is, in at least two meaningful senses, a "derived reality."

First, the situations, in particular the characters and settings, found in the vast majority (12/13 or 92.3% in 1990, and 9/14 or 64.3% in 1992) of the programs analyzed were adapted from other media—books, movies, famous personalities, video games, comics, and other TV shows (see Table 5.1). It might be argued, then, that the social reality depicted on Saturday mornings is largely serendipitous—that is, it is the haphazard amalgamation of the cartoon adaptations of previously contrived situations. Two observations, however, suggest otherwise.

To begin with, it is obvious that any adaptation process is highly selective, and thus the materials selected for adaptation as Saturday morning cartoons were selected precisely for their popularity with young audiences and their (not unrelated) "fit" with established Saturday morning formulae. Second, most of the cartoon adaptations we looked at included changes in social reality elements favoring the same such formulae. For example, the setting in the cartoon version of *Beetlejuice* is suburban, not rural as in the movie. *Beetlejuice* the cartoon also focuses on an adolescent character who was less central to the plot of the movie, diminishes the adult characters, who were more central, and adds several adolescent characters not present at all in the movie version. Even more telling, perhaps, is the fact that the plots of these cartoon adaptations bear little, if any, resemblance to those of the material from which they came. They rather resemble nothing so much as each other.

Table 5.1. Derivation of Saturday Morning Cartoons.

Classification	Sept 15, 1990		June 9, 1992	
	Number	Percent	Number	Percent
Comic	2/13**	15.4%	2/14**	14.4%
Book	2/13*	15.4%	1/14*	7.1%
Movie	3/13	23.0%	3/14	21.5%
TV show	2/13	15.4%	1/14	7.1%
Video game	1/13	7.7%	1/14	7.1%
Personalities	2/13	15.4%	1/14	7.1%
Total Derived	12/13	92.3%	9/14	64.3%
Total Original	1/13	7.7%	5/14	35.7%

*are also movies
**Teenage Mutant Ninja Turtles was also later made into a series of movies

A second important way in which the social reality found in Saturday morning programming is a derived reality involves the formal properties of animated cartoons themselves. It is simply that animated cartoons are derived versions of traditional film and video, more iconic and less realistic renditions of regular television fare. It might therefore be suggested that children are less likely to view cartoons as "real," (Dorr, 1986), hence children are less likely to internalize the social reality they portray. The latter is most probably not true.

Iconic images simplify reality. They strip what they represent to their essential qualities, making these easier, not harder to assimilate. In addition, iconic images invite participation; their very lack of specificity encourages viewers to identify with cartoon characters (McCloud, 1994). It can be argued, therefore, that the derived formal reality of Saturday morning cartoons is especially well constructed for children to begin learning about the larger society in which they find themselves, and to begin developing notions of their place in it.

This chapter is divided into four parts, each of which explores a different dimension of social reality as seen through the derived reality of Saturday morning programming. The first considers the age, ethnic, and gender makeup of cartoon characters, and the effects those depictions might have on children's developing notions of their larger world. The second is concerned with the workings of that larger world as portrayed in the settings and plots found in Saturday morning programming. The third examines the morals and values expressed in the themes of Saturday morning cartoons and compares these with the morals and values expressed in the themes of such traditional children's stories as fairy tales, fables, and myths. The fourth deals with Saturday morning commercials and commercialism. It looks not only at the commercials aired during Saturday morning programming, but at the pervasive marketing of products based on the programs themselves.

AGE, ETHNICITY, AND GENDER

The characters found in Saturday morning cartoons, even the talking animals, can be seen to have obvious ages and genders. They are old or young, male or female. Many cartoon characters, the human ones at least, also have an obvious ethnicity. These age, ethnic, and gender depictions in Saturday morning programming impact young viewers' developing conceptions of social reality in important ways.

Most important, perhaps, is that when one sort of person is portrayed over and over again in a particular way, such depictions can contribute to the development of stereotypes. For example, if old men are repeatedly portrayed as incompetent (as is indeed the case in Saturday morning programming), viewers of these portrayals will come to believe that old men are incompetent, especially when they have had little personal exposure to old men themselves. Once embraced, such stereotypes are hard to dislodge. If, for example, a child has come to think old men are incompetent, he or she will tend to perceive them that way, regardless of the reality.

Gerbner (Gerbner, Gross, Morgan & Signorielli, 1980) likened the effects of stereotypic television portrayals on developing notions of what differing groups of people are like to the cumulative effects of cultivation on a crop. He also argued that, although a single viewing of a particular kind of person portrayed in a particular way will have little effect on viewers' images of that sort of person, when one sort of person is depicted again and again as having the same characteristics, viewers will begin to believe that all people of that sort share such characteristics. Similarly, the cumulative effects of viewing particular kinds of people over and over again in the same kinds of roles can strongly impact the developing child's notions of their own and others' places in the world.

To analyze age, ethnic, and gender depictions in Saturday morning cartoons, each program appearing between 8:00 a.m. and 11:00 a.m. on September 15, 1990 and June 9, 1992 was viewed, and all its major characters listed on a rating sheet. Raters were asked to give each character's ethnicity, gender, and age, and to tell whether the character was portrayed as good or evil, as competent or incompetent, and as being in a position of authority or not. Two raters reviewed each program and discrepancies between ratings were resolved by the author with reference to the program tapes. In this manner, a total of 123 characters were identified as appearing in the programs aired on September 15, 1990, and a total of 105 characters were found in the programs aired on June 9, 1992 (Knowles & Swan, 1992). All of the characters identified could be classified in terms of age and gender; thus all were included in those analyses. Many characters, however, had to be discounted when considering ethnicity, either because they definitely had no ethnicity (dogs, cats, aliens, etc.), or because their ethnicity was dubious. In terms of ethnicity, therefore, only 61 of 123 (49.5%; 1990) and 91 of 105 (86.6%; 1992) characters could be studied.

The relative ages of the characters found in the Saturday morning cartoons we reviewed are summarized in Table 5.2. It shows that the demographics of these programs were skewed toward young characters, although a good deal less so in 1992 than in 1990. Such findings are neither surprising nor, in themselves, disturbing. It makes sense to overpopulate cartoons with young characters with whom young viewers can identify. The extremely low representation of older people in cartoons, however, is unrealistic and perhaps emblematic of American society's increasing propensity to separate senior citizens from its mainstream. Even more disturbing is that the very few older characters we found in both 1990 and 1992 were depicted as either incompetent or evil. Indeed, the general trend we saw in the characterizations of both years would suggest that the older the character, the more likely they are to be either evil or incompetent or both. This is clearly not a healthy message to impart, intended or not.

Table 5.2. Age of Saturday Morning Cartoon Characters.

Classification	Sept 15, 1990		June 9, 1992	
	Number	Percent	Number	Percent
Total young	92/123	74.8%	60/105	57.1%
Total adult	27/123	21.9%	42/105	40.0%
Total old	4/123	3.3%	3/105	2.9%

Table 5.3 gives a summary of the ethnicity of the characters found in Saturday morning cartoons. In 1990, of the characters whose ethnicity could be determined, 32% belonged to ethnic minorities, most of whom were Black. Although this might, on the surface, appear to be a good representation, a full 60% of the total minorities represented (12/20) were found on a single show, *Kid 'N Play*, which was an all-minority show about a rap group. The remaining minority group characters in 1990 included two female Black teenagers in *Camp Candy*, Luigi and Julio Mario (who are

Table 5.3. Ethnicity by Gender of Saturday Morning Cartoon Characters.

Classification	Sept. 15, 1990 Number	Percent	June 9, 1992 Number	Percent
Black female	2/61	3.2%	2/91	2.2%
Black male	12/61	19.2%	8/91	8.8%
Total Black	14/61	22.4%	10/91	11.0%
Hispanic male	3/61	4.8%	0/91	0.0%
Hispanic female	0/61	0.0%	1/91	1.1%
Total Hispanic	3/61	4.8%	1/91	1.1%
Asian male	0/61	0.0%	1/91	1.1%
Asian female	0/61	0.0%	1/91	1.1%
Total Asian	0/61	0.0%	2/91	2.2%
Italian male	2/61	4.8%	2/91	2.2%
Total other	2/61	4.8%	2/91	2.2%
Total Minorities	20/61	32.0%	15/91	16.5%

Italian) in *Captain N and Super Mario Brothers,* and four Black males given token supporting roles on other programs. Almost half the cartoons we reviewed from 1990 had no minority representation at all.

Luigi and Julio Mario made the ethnic count again in 1992, where, without the ghetto of *Kid 'N Play,* minority representation was down to 16.5%, and, again, fully half the shows had no minority representation at all. The majority of ethnic characters, and the only variety therein, were found on *Captain Planet and the Planeteers,* which took pains to include Black, Asian, and Hispanic characters. Other ethnic characters found in 1992 included two Black males with leading roles in Pro Stars (how could a show based on famous athletes not include Black men?); the rest were token Black roles in *Ghostbusters, Saved by the Bell, Wish Kid,* and an updated *Yo, Yogi.*

It would seem, then, that Saturday morning cartoons are a lot like American society. They have their own ethnic ghettos, and, with the exception of a few shows, give only token representation to ethnic minorities outside these. Although this may indeed reflect power relationships in the larger society, it does not reflect the America many of us would like to see. If we would have our children create a better, more integrated America, shouldn't we be presenting them with images of what such a world might be like? Perhaps more importantly, shouldn't we be presenting minority children with role models other than athletes and rap performers to which they can aspire? In this vein, it is also important to note that, except for the characters in *Kid 'N Play* and *Pro Stars* based on real people, the minority characters we found in Saturday morning cartoons tended to lack ethnicity, rather, they were darker, Spanish-speaking versions of middle-class Whites.

One of the most disappointing findings in our analyses of minority representation in cartoon programming concerns the number of Black female roles, 2/61 (3.2%) in 1990 and 2/91 (2.2%) in 1992. It is even more disappointing when one realizes that these two singular characters were found together in the same program in both years (*Camp Candy* in 1990; *Yo, Yogi* in 1992). There were also no older minority characters in the programming we studied, nor was a member of an ethnic minority portrayed as evil. Although it may be the case that it is still important to portray minorities exclusively as "nice" people, the figures for Black females and the total lack of older ethnic characters seem unjustifiable in terms of the actual demographics of the American population.

In terms of the actual demographics of the American population, the general gender representation we found in Saturday morning programming (summarized in Table 5.4) is clearly also unjustifiable. Female characters were much more evenly distributed across the programs studied than were minority characters, but the total representation of female characters (17.8% in 1990 and 23.8% in 1992) was very disappointing. Considering that females account for more than 50% of the population at large, this is a serious imbalance. Interestingly, proportionately more females than males were rated as generally competent, although, by proportion, slightly more males than females were found in positions of authority. Again, although this may mirror power relations in the real world, it cannot really be the case that we want to socialize our young girls to expect and/or accept such conditions.

Table 5.4. Gender by Age of Saturday Morning Cartoon Characters.

Classification	Sept 15, 1990		June 9, 1992	
	Number	Percent	Number	Percent
Young female	15/123	12.2%	13/105	12.4%
Adult female	5/123	4.0%	11/105	10.4%
Old female	2/123	1.6%	1/105	1.0%
Total Female	22/123	17.8%	25/105	23.8%
Young male	77/123	62.8%	47/105	44.8%
Adult male	22/123	17.8%	31/105	29.5%
Old male	2/1231	1.6%	2/105	1.9%
Total Male	101/123	82.2%	80/105	76.2%

In 1990, the portrayal of women in the programs we reviewed was generally stereotypical. Apart from Dorothy in *The Wizard of Oz*, Lydia in *Beetlejuice*, and Miss Piggy in the *Muppet Babies*, female cartoon characters played supporting roles. Lydia and Miss Piggy, moreover, are not very sympathetic characters (Miss Piggy is pushy and violent; Lydia is odd) and Dorothy, although ostensibly the major character, remained tangential to the storylines and the action in *The Wizard of Oz*. Like Dorothy, the supporting female characters found in 1990 cartoons were all very "nice," and all quite tangential to the stories. These characters were almost uniformly pretty, tended to be concerned about their appearance, and were generally taken care of by male characters. There was a high proportion of princesses.

In 1992, the situation regarding the stereotyping of women in cartoon programming was recognizably better. Although there were still princesses and stereotypical supporting female characters, an effort was made (especially in action/adventure shows) to include at least one female character who participated fully in the action of a storyline and/or who held a position of authority. Nonetheless, all the group leaders and all the central protagonists (except for the indefatigable Lydia) in the 1992 programming were male, and male characters still outnumbered female characters by more than three to one. This undeniable and continuing underrepresentation must be having some effect on young girls. That males still overwhelmingly dominate the cast of cartoon characters socializes all children to believe they somehow "deserve" greater social recognition and status. At the very least, equal numbers of male and female characters should populate Saturday morning cartoons.

SETTINGS AND PLOTS

Children's developing conceptions of social reality are not only impacted by character depictions in Saturday morning cartoons, but by the ways in which society in general is portrayed. Important elements in determining this latter category are setting and plot.

By most definitions, the term *setting* encompasses both place and time. In either respect, settings can be further differentiated as either *integral* or *backdrop* (Donelson & Nilsen, 1989). An integral setting is one that is highly specified and an essential part of the plot itself, as in the case of many fantasies and historical stories. In *The Wizard of Oz*, for example, the setting is almost a character itself. Backdrop settings, on the other hand, are undifferentiated and generalized. When authors establish this kind of setting, they are interested in creating a neutral backdrop for their stories, to make it easier for readers to identify with and participate in its action.

The vast majority of settings in the Saturday morning cartoons we reviewed were of the latter, background, variety (see Table 5.5). Except for a part of one segment in the *Muppet Babies,* none of the cartoons we reviewed were set in a specific time. Rather, all, as evidenced by dialogue, characterizations, and props, seemed to take place in an indeterminate present. Only 5 of the 21 different programs reviewed over both years (3 shown in 1990 and 5 shown in 1992) were set in a specific location. These 5 included the *New Adventures of Winnie the Pooh, The Wizard of Oz, Captain 'N and Super Mario Brothers, Yo, Yogi,* and *Land of the Lost*; programs, it could be argued, adapted from original material in which place was too important to be homogenized. It should also be noted that with the exception of *Yo, Yogi's* "Jellystone Park," all these settings are fantastic (Bokan, 1992).

The common use of background settings in the Saturday morning programming we reviewed would seem to indicate that its creators were more interested in developing a sense of immediacy and generality then in setting their stories in a particular place and time. Deliberate vagueness or stereotyping of setting allows viewers to fill in gaps with personal experience and more closely involve themselves in the action of the characters. The use of backdrop settings in Saturday morning programming, then, like the iconic nature of its characters, adds to the likelihood that the social reality depicted therein will be internalized and assimilated. Indeed, in the majority of the cartoon programs we reviewed, physical setting merely provided generalized parameters in which their action took place.

To examine such parameters a little more closely, program raters were asked to distinguish the settings of each program segment as rural, suburban, urban, or fantastic (Bokan, 1992). Because many of the cartoons we reviewed contained fantastic elements—monsters, robots, dinosaurs, and so on—a cartoon setting was deemed fantastic only when the setting itself would not exist in the real world. The physical surroundings in *Captain N and Super Mario,* for example, are the inner workings of video games, a fairly fantastic premise. Similarly, *Winnie the Pooh* takes place in a realm of stuffed animals. Although the settings of both these programs are formally vaguely rural, the premises establishing them are

Table 5.5. Specificity of Settings in Saturday Morning Cartoons.

Classification	Sept.15, 1990		June 9, 1992	
	Number	Percent	Number	Percent
Integral settings	3/13	23.1%	5/14	35.7%
Background settings	10/13	76.9%	9/1	64.3%

essentially fantastic. On the other hand, *Slimer and the Real Ghostbusters* contains many fantastic characters, but its settings and the premises that underlie them are essentially urban. Finally, in *Beetlejuice*, we found two distinct settings—the ghoulish "Beetleworld," and the suburban Peaceful Pines. *Beetlejuice* was therefore listed once as having a fantastic setting, and once as having a suburban setting.

To take into consideration, however, the fantastic elements that we did find in many Saturday morning programs, raters were additionally asked to note these. For these purposes, fantastic elements were considered to be magical, monstrous, and/or mechanical entities, and not the talking animals who commonly populate cartoons. Two raters reviewed each program and no discrepancies between ratings were found. The results of the rating process are summarized in Table 5.6.

The results of our analyses of cartoon settings are perhaps most interesting in the changes they show over time. In 1990, cartoon settings were predominantly urban and fantastic; in 1992, they were predominantly suburban and fantastic. There was also a decided growth in programs featuring fantastical elements over this 2-year period. Such findings suggest a retreat to the suburbs and the fantastic, and, by implication, a corresponding fear of cities. Indeed, by 1992, the only two shows with urban settings were *Slimer and the Real Ghostbusters* and *Teenage Mutant Ninja Turtles*, shows in which urban landscapes take on a decidedly sinister quality and the main characters live in fortress-like headquarters from which they emerge only to fight urban evil.

The settings of Saturday morning cartoons, therefore, would seem to suggest to children that one lives in the suburbs, dreams of the country, and fears the city. Indeed, such notions, however unrealistic, are probably a part of the American psyche in general. It is nonetheless dis-

Table 5.6. Settings in Saturday Morning Cartoons.

Classification	Sept. 15, 1990		June 9, 1992	
	Number*	Percent	Number*	Percent
Rural	2/14	14.3%	3^1/15	20.0%
Suburban	2/14	14.3%	5^2/15	33.3%
Urban	6^3/14	42.8%	2^2/15	13.4%
Fantastic	4/14	28.6%	5/15	33.3%
Total fantastic or fantastic elem.	7/14	50.0%	10/15	66.7%

*Total numbers of shows include Beetlejuice counted both as suburban and fantastical; superscripts indicate numbers of shows in a category whose settings include fantastical elements.

turbing, however, because of the background nature of cartoon settings and the nature of their audience. As previously stated, children have little knowledge or experience of the larger world. When that larger world is presented to them in generalized forms that over and over again associate cities with evil, chances are they will internalize such associations, most likely at deep levels. In a similar vein, the growing number of fantastic (and scary) elements in Saturday morning programming cannot help but increase children's generalized fears of the larger world.

Another element in Saturday morning cartoons that effects their portrayal of society is the general nature of their plot structures. Of all the elements in a cartoon, plot is probably most variable, but the very simplicity of form found in Saturday morning programs makes it possible to draw some conclusions about the nature of their plots. One particular distinction that can be made concerning cartoon plots seems especially relevant to the concepts of social reality they portray. This is a distinction between *action/adventure* and *situational* plots. Program raters were asked to note such differences, and again no discrepancies were found between raters.

Table 5.7 distinguishes between cartoons whose plot structures were based on an action/adventure model and cartoons whose plot structures were situationally grounded. Cartoon plots were considered action/adventure when their structures centered on violent threats to society, usually in the form of fantastical monsters or machines, that were neutralized through the violent actions of the cartoon's heroes. Plots considered situational were those that revolved around everyday situations. Whether comedic or dramatic, situational plots were generally set in motion by misunderstandings and/or misguided actions, or by contests or conflicts between characters, and typically ended with a simple moral message.

Differences between the kinds of plots found in Saturday morning programming, like differences in settings, are most interesting when viewed over time. They also reveal similar trends. In 1990, situational plots were common to nearly twice as many programs as action/adven-

Table 5.7. Kinds of Plots in Saturday Morning Cartoons.

Classification	Sept 15, 1990		June 9, 1992	
	Number*	Percent	Number*	Percent
Action/adventure	5/14	35.7%	9/15	60.0%
Situational (comedy/drama)	9/14	64.3%	6/15	40.0%

*total numbers of shows include *Beetlejuice* counted both as action/adventure and situational in both years.

ture plots. In 1992, action/adventure plots outnumbered situational ones by 50%. It would appear that society as portrayed in cartoons got a good deal meaner and scarier between 1990 and 1992. Cartoon society also got more violent and more ready to accept violence as a solution to social problems. Such portrayal only exasperates children's fears. What is even more disturbing about this trend is its movement away from concepts of personal responsibility (i.e., character flaws can get you into trouble; personal strengths can get you out) and toward notions of victimization. Although all these tendencies may mirror similar changes in the larger society, it is hard to believe they are positive in either arena. Indeed, it could be easily argued that presenting such images to children only insures that the trends will continue.

VALUES AND MORALITY

The work of childhood is learning to be a member of the culture in which one finds him or herself. In the previous sections of this chapter, we explored cartoon portrayals of what could be called the surface features of modern American culture—what Saturday morning cartoons are teaching children about everyday relations in the larger world. In this section and the next, we examine cartoon treatments of the belief systems—the currents, if you will—that underlie and support that surface.

Stories have always been a primary means through which the values and beliefs of peoples have been passed from generation to generation. Consider, for example, Aesop's fables, or Nordic myth, or the parables of the New Testament. This is not to say that children do not learn values and mores primarily from their immediate families, or that individual families do not pass along to their children their own particular interpretations of the same, but rather that the larger culture encodes its values and beliefs in stories which are passed from generation to generation. Once upon a time, these stories were passed down by village storytellers and traveling bards. With the advent of print, they were set and reset in books, the stories being changed and updated for succeeding generations. Today, 75% of the American population gets the majority of its information from television, and 40% of American homes have no books at all (Costanzo, 1994). The average American child of today spends far more time with the stories found on Saturday morning cartoons than with the books—the fairy tales, fables, myths, and historical stories—that were an important part of my childhood.

Indeed, it is important to note that the messages of Saturday morning cartoons have evolved in conscious recognition of this fact. The cartoons of the 1950s and 1960s were little more than slapstick routines made more violent by the immortal nature of animated talent (consider, for example, *Bugs Bunny, Daffy Duck,* the *Road Runner, Tom and Jerry,* even *Huckleberry Hound*). It is precisely because concerned parents and educators recognized the growing cultural importance of Saturday morning programming and put pressure on broadcasters to produce "socially responsible" cartoons (Kaye, 1979) that the kinds of stories found in today's programming were developed. Thus, the social reality depicted in Saturday morning cartoons is also "derived" in this sense; its moral messages were to a greater or lesser extent engineered in response to public pressure.

To analyze the values and belief systems expounded in the stories found in Saturday morning programming, program raters were asked to summarize the plots of all the stories in each program they reviewed, and to note the primary and secondary themes embedded therein in terms of the values they seemed to support. Two raters reviewed each program and discrepancies between judgments were resolved by the author with reference to the program tapes (Guadagno & Swan, 1992).

So what are the stories found in Saturday morning programming like? In many ways, these stories are very similar to traditional fairy tales and fables—they tend to combine realistic problems with fantastic solutions; they explore both specific ethical dilemmas and the nature of good and evil itself; they are populated with talking animals, monsters, and magic. In many ways, what we have called situational plots resembled those of traditional fables. They tended to have very simple structures that focused on a particular social message, often explored through humor, and most could be summed up with an aphorism (i.e., "courage comes from within," "bigger is not always better," "things are not always what they seem"). Similarly, what we have called action/adventure plots in many ways resembled traditional myths and fairy tales. They were uniformly concerned with threats to society itself, usually in monstrous form, which were defeated by heroic action and magic powers. In many ways, however, the stories we found in Saturday morning cartoons were quite different from those found in traditional children's stories, and, in many ways, these differences are what is most interesting about them.

The biggest difference between classic children's stories, between the cartoons we remember from our childhoods, for that matter, and the Saturday morning cartoons of today, involves quite a dramatic change from an individual to a group focus. Classic children's stories focus on individual protagonists. In traditional fairy tales and myths, the plots follow individual heroes and their struggles to save society and "find" themselves. Traditional fables typically deal with character traits as embodied in individual characters.

To explore differences in focus in cartoon stories, program raters were asked to distinguish between programs whose stories had an individual focus and those whose stories had a group focus. There were no discrepancies between raters. Table 5.8 summarizes their findings. It shows that in both 1990 and 1992, the overwhelming majority of cartoons plots, more than three quarters of these in both years, were focused on the behaviors of groups.

In all of the action/adventure cartoons we reviewed, good was embodied in a group of more or less equals, not in an individual. In all, it was through the collective action of such heroes that evil was defeated and society restored, and more often than not, it was attempts at solitary action that got the whole group into trouble in the first place. Good in Saturday morning cartoons is democratic. Conversely, evil in action/adventure cartoons we reviewed was embodied in an individual, albeit sometimes an individual with stooges. The villains of the cartoons we watched were typically isolated from society. If they were several, there was always a single autocratic leader, the "embodiment of evil" so to speak, and many mindless underlings. Evil on Saturday mornings is not democratic.

In terms of actions, however, there was little to distinguish heroes from villains in these programs. The villains used trickery, violence, intelligence, and magic to try to take over society and destroy the heroes; the heroes used trickery, violence, intelligence, and magic to defeat them. Although all of the action/adventure cartoon plots we reviewed seemed to have a good-versus-evil theme, neither good nor evil was clearly distinguished in terms of particular character traits of their heroes or villains, nor were such behaviors plot devices. The heroes of Saturday morning did not possess good character traits (i.e., faith, pureness of heart, charity, etc.) that were responsible for their eventual triumph. Likewise, the villains were not motivated by character flaws (i.e., jealousy, greed, lust, etc.). At most, Saturday morning villains seemed to want power for its own sake, whereas its heroes were content to share power.

Indeed, even the stories in cartoons with what we have termed situational plots—even the stories in those very few cartoons we thought still preserved an individual focus through strong characterizations (i.e., *Garfield and Friends, Beetlejuice, Yo Yogi,* and *Muppet Babies*)—were essentially stories about groups and group relationships. Most often, all these situ-

Table 5.8. Unit Focus in Saturday Morning Cartoons.

Classification	Sept 15, 1990		June 9, 1992	
	Number	Percent	Number	Percent
Individual focus	3/13	23.1%	3/14	21.5%
Group focus	10/13	76.9%	11/14	78.5%

ational stories revolved around primary themes of friendship, loyalty, and cooperation—group values. We also found a variety of what might be called *secondary themes* in the cartoons we examined. One recurrent secondary theme concerned the importance of education; another involved careful thinking (i.e., "don't jump to conclusions," "think out the consequences of your actions"). Other secondary themes we discerned included good sportsmanship, courage, kindness, responsibility, self-worth, persistence, and concern for the environment.

These various secondary themes and the values they emphasized were positive ones that we would want instilled in our children, and, unlike plot development in action/adventure stories, they were central to situational plots. Because of the secondary nature of such positive character portrayals, however, and because they tended to be developed within stories that were primarily concerned with group relationships, individual values and individualism itself were at best ignored. At worst, individualism seemed portrayed as a negative character trait. As was the case in their action/adventure counterparts, the more negative characters in situational cartoons tended to act alone, and group members frequently got themselves into trouble by doing the same.

An interesting contrast, however, can be observed between the group dominated messages of Saturday morning cartoons and the public service messages embedded in cartoon programming (Meurs & Griffis, 1992). The public service messages in the programming we reviewed were produced by both the networks and outside agencies. They were generally 15- to 30-second spots, mixed in with commercials during program breaks, that focused on many of the same topics as the secondary themes in the cartoon programs themselves—the importance of education, self-worth, concern for the environment, and so on.

What was interesting about these messages was that their primary thrust, in direct contrast with that of the cartoons with which they were shown, involved individual responsibility. Messages about drugs, for example, focused on not giving in to peer pressure; environmental and safety messages emphasized the differences an individual can make; what we termed social messages concerned "being yourself." It must be remembered that these public service messages accounted for less than 7 minutes out of 9 hours of programming time. Nevertheless, they stand in curious contrast to the group-dominated themes of the cartoons themselves. A complete category breakdown of public service messages is shown in Table 5.9.

Another big difference between Saturday morning cartoons and classic children's stories is the former's lack of a sense of history. Classic children's literature has always included not only allusions to historical characters and events, but historical stories themselves. Among the well-remembered stories of my own childhood, for example, were American

Table 5.9. Public Service Messages in Saturday Morning Cartoons.

Classification	Sept 15, 1990		June 9, 1992	
	Number	Percent	Number	Percent
School/reading	5	31.3%	8	42.1%
Nutrition	2	12.5%	3	15.8%
Drugs	2	12.5%	2	10.5%
Social	2	12.5%	0	0.0%
Safety	1	6.2%	5	26.3%
Environment	2	12.5%	0	0.0%
Community agencies	2	12.5%	1	5.3%
Total Messages	16	100.0%	19	100.0%

stories—some mythical (i.e., John Henry, Paul Bunyan, Rip Van Winkle), some historical (i.e., the Boston Tea Party, Appomattox, Prince Joseph), some a little of both (Johnnie Appleseed, George Washington and the cherry tree, Harriet Tubman).

There are no American stories, there aren't even any characters from or allusions to them, or any other history for that matter, in Saturday morning cartoons. This complete lack of any sense of history is another radical departure from traditional children's literature, even from the cartoons of the past. It is also, I believe, a serious failing in Saturday morning programming. A people's history is an important part of their culture. What better way to teach values and beliefs than to embed them in historical stories? Perhaps Saturday morning cartoon's lack of a sense of the past stems from their derived nature, from their engineering. Perhaps they lack historical sense because they lack a history themselves. On the other hand, it may be that in this respect, too, Saturday morning cartoons simply reflect the larger culture, which similarly seems to be loosing its sense of history.

A final significant difference between traditional children's stories and Saturday morning cartoons is that traditional stories, fairy tales in particular, address psychological issues of special importance to the developing child. In *The Uses of Enchantment,* Bruno Bettelheim (1976) argued that what children urgently need from their stories are not lessons in cooperative behavior, but the assurance that they can succeed; that monsters can be slain, injustice remedied, obstacles overcome. Fairy tales, he maintains, give children this assurance precisely because their fantastic dangers are rooted in a child's worst psychological fears—the fear of being abandoned, the fear of powerful adults, the fear of their own negative impulses. When the protagonists of such epics face and dramatically defeat those dangers, their audience vicariously learns that they can overcome and defeat their own fearfulness. Saturday morning cartoons, even the action/adventure type programs that on the surface seem to resemble fairy tales, fail to meet a child's psychological needs for two important reasons.

First, they fail to address children's real fears. Threats to society are an adult issue—a child's issues involve threats to him- or herself. In addition, an important part of a child's fears are the isolation he or she feels in the face of them. The heroes of fairy tales struggle alone to overcome evil, and so reassure children that they can overcome their fears. The group-dominated plots of action/adventure cartoons, especially their repeated suggestion that solitary individuals can never by themselves overcome evil, can only serve to increase such fears.

Second, unlike fairy-tale endings, the endings of Saturday morning cartoons hold no real punishment for the wicked. In action/adventure stories, evil doers are, at best, sent back to some other dimension; at worst, they escape to terrorize the heroes again. In like manner, the endings of Saturday morning action/adventure cartoons hold no real rewards for their heroes; their lives just return to conditions as they were at the beginning of the story. Similarly, in situational plots, negative characters and/or actions are merely frustrated, and the only rewards are lessons learned. Bettelheim (1976) argued that, for children, only severe punishment fits the crimes they believe have been committed against them, and only substantial benefits can adequately reward their heroic efforts to prevail. In the prosocial world of Saturday morning cartoons, there is no real punishment, no real rewards; hence, no justice. If Bettelheim is right, the message that there is no justice in the world cannot be one we want to be sending our children.

In any case, the overwhelming message, the ubiquitous moral in the Saturday morning programming we examined was that acting with the group is good, acting on your own is evil. Karp (1987) wrote:

> In every conceivable way, children are taught the pro-social virtues of cooperation, self-effacement, and subservience to the group. . . . [The] message is perfectly plain: The lone individual is weak and helpless; the group is strong and kind. (pp. 439-440)

Karp went on to argue that Saturday morning programming is thus:

> systematic training for personal weakness and social subservience. It promotes conformity and saps inner strength. It teaches the children of a free people to look to the group for their opinions and to despise those who do not do the same. (p. 444)

Karp, of course, is exaggerating to make a point, but he does have one. Clearly, the cooperative group values espoused in Saturday morning cartoons can be very positive, especially when viewed against the kinds of violent and aggressive behaviors psychologists have found to result from the viewing of violent, aggressive, and highly individualistic cartoons. In addition, the associations between democratic groups and good, and autocratic individuals and evil developed in Saturday morning programming can be seen as fostering democratic behaviors. On the other hand, submission to a group is not always positive; consider, for example, Nazi Germany, street gangs, or some of the more radical religious communities in this country today. Group-related values, especially in a democracy, need to be balanced against individual responsibility and respect for the individual—something that was done very little, if at all, in the themes of Saturday morning programs we examined.

For well or ill, such group-dominated messages are a radical departure both from Western storytelling tradition, in which the hero typically embarks on a solitary quest to rescue society and/or prove his or her character, and the traditional American ethos of rugged individualism. That it was also a conscious departure is yet another difference between classic children's stories and the stories found in Saturday morning cartoons. Perhaps the real problem here is that Saturday morning cartoons never truly evolved into classic children's stories in the first place, but were rather engineered according to artificial codes, however well intentioned, into pseudo-stories. Perhaps they may yet evolve to messier but richer and more classic forms. On the other hand, perhaps the group-dominated messages of Saturday morning cartoons are merely a reflection of the corporate models that dominate so much of our advanced capitalist society. Perhaps such messages, like ethnic and gender depictions in cartoons, merely reflect power relationships in the world as it is.

CONSUMERISM

The previous section of this chapter explored the values and belief systems embedded in and communicated through the stories developed in Saturday morning cartoons. This section examines the ways in which Saturday morning programming itself supports the consumerism that lies at the very heart of our culture.

The United States boasts the most fully developed commercial broadcasting system in the world. It is paid for, and so to a greater or lesser degree controlled by, companies that manufacture and sell commercial products. What they are buying is increased consumer demand for their wares; Saturday morning programming is no exception. Can children effectively defend themselves against the impact of commercials? Many researchers in the field think not. Goldberg and Gorn (1983), for example, have established a causal link between children's exposure to an advertised product and their efforts to obtain it, and, more importantly perhaps, between children's exposure to advertising and other generalized purchase related behaviors. The more television children watch, they report, the more stuff they want. The National Institute of Mental Health's (1982) survey of research on children and advertising supports such claim.

Findings such as these have led groups like Action for Children's Television (Kaye, 1979) to campaign long and hard for rules governing advertising in Saturday morning programming. These efforts led to the passage of the Children's Television Act of 1990, which limits the amount of time that can be devoted to commercial messages in Saturday morning programming to 2 minutes per half hour. However, is this time limit *enough* of a limit? Is it really possible to take commercialism out of children's programming in a system so ubiquitously commercial? For that matter, do we really want to? To begin exploring some of these issues, all the commercial messages shown between 8:00 a.m. and 11:00 a.m. on all three major television networks on Saturday, September 15, 1990 and again on Saturday, June 9, 1992 (after the Children's Television Act took effect) were recorded and categorized. These findings (Greenless & Swan, 1992) are summarized in Table 5.10.

In 1990, commercial messages accounted for a little more than 5 minutes out of every half hour of the Saturday morning programming we reviewed. In that year, we counted 185 commercials broadcast during the 9 hours of cartoon programs we watched. The average number of repetitions of a particular commercial was three. In 1992, advertisers were limited to 2 minutes of commercial messages in every half hour of Saturday morning programming. In that year, we counted 161 commercials broad-

Table 5.10. Commercials in Saturday Morning Cartoons.

Classification	Sept 15, 1990 Number	Sept 15, 1990 Percent	June 9, 1992 Number	June 9, 1992 Percent
Sugar foods & beverages	67	36.2%	75	46.6%
Junk food	19	10.3%	39	24.2%
Total other foods	10	5.4%	15	9.3%
Total food & beverages	96	51.9%	129	80.1%
Toys	70	37.8%	17	10.6%
Entertainment	14	7.6%	15	9.3%
Other	5	2.7%	0	0.0%
Total Messages	185	100.0%	161	100.0%

cast during the 9 hours of cartoon programs we watched. The average number of repetitions of a particular commercial was three. In addition, the number of transitions, and so the number of different images shown within individual commercials, also remained essentially unchanged across these 2 years. Thus we found that the Children's Television Act did very little to change the numbers of commercial messages with which children are bombarded on Saturday mornings. What happened was that advertisers simply compressed their messages from 30 seconds to 15 seconds, speeding up the images contained therein accordingly. It did, however, result in changes in the content of those messages.

In 1990, food and beverage commercials accounted for a little more than half the total number of commercials shown; commercials for toys accounted for the bulk of the remaining commercials, almost 40% of the total. In 1992, food and beverage commercials accounted for 80% of the total number of commercials shown, and commercials for toys had fallen to just 10% of the total. Thus, whereas before the Children's Television Act went into effect there were almost as many toy commercials as food and beverage commercials shown during Saturday morning programming, after it went into effect, food and beverage commercials accounted for the overwhelming majority of commercials. Although the absolute numbers of commercials shown during that time period dropped slightly, the absolute numbers of commercials for food and beverages rose by fully one third.

My guess is that the reason for these changes is simply that advertisements for toys are not as easily compressed as advertisements for food and beverages. Toy commercials typically show a toy and what can be done with it. This requires more camera movement, longer cuts, and more time than commercials for food and beverages, which traditionally have had little to do with the products themselves and could therefore be more easily altered. The changes themselves, however, are problematic when one considers the kinds of food and beverage advertising shown during Saturday morning cartoons. In both 1990 and 1992, only about 10% of the food and beverage advertising shown during that period was for foods I would consider nutritious (Table 5.11).

Table 5.11 shows that only 10 of the 96 food and beverage commercials shown in 1990, and only 15 of the 129 food and beverage commercials shown in 1992 were for foods we considered at all nutritious. The rest were for foods high in sugar and fat. Poor eating habits, dental cavities, and obesity are serious health problems children carry into their adult lives. Poor nutrition has immediate effects on children as well, contributing to such problems as hyperactivity, fatigue, and attention deficits that effect their progress in school. However, on every network, children were shown commercials pushing products that foster poor nutrition an average of 9 times per hour in 1990, and an average of 13 times an hour

Table 5.11. Food and Beverage Commercials in Saturday Morning Cartoons.

Classification	Sept. 15, 1990 Number	Sept. 15, 1990 Percent	June 9, 1992 Number	June 9, 1992 Percent
Sugared beverages	19	19.8%	7	5.4%
Cookies & candy	12	12.5%	9	7.0%
Sugar cereals	36	37.5%	59	45.7%
Total sugar foods	67	69.8%	75	58.1%
Other cereals	3	3.1%	1	0.7%
Snacks	7	7.3%	6	4.7%
Fast food	12	12.5%	33	25.6%
Total junk food	19	19.8%	39	30.3%
Other foods	7	7.3%	14	10.9%
Total sugar & junk foods	86	89.6%	114	88.4%
Total nutritious foods	10	10.4%	15	11.6
Total food & beverages	96	100.0%	129	100.0%

in 1992. In 1992, those commercials made up the vast majority of advertising shown on Saturday mornings; the bad nutrition message wasn't even broken up with commercials for toys.

Well, one might say, at least the number of commercials for toys were down. Or were they really? The fact is that all but one of the cartoon programs shown on Saturday mornings in both 1990 and 1992 were associated with series toys and all sorts of other commercial products for children—lunch boxes, pencil sets, night lights, games, clothing, even books. Series toys, however, are the most insidious. These are toys that have many different figures and "playsets," each with their own differing accessories. The *Beetlejuice* series, for example, not only offers many different figures and playsets, it offers seven different Beetlejuices. Each of the packages says, "Collect them all!" Only someone who hasn't been in a toy store in the last 5 years could have missed the *Teenage Mutant Ninja Turtles* series; it takes up a whole aisle. Series toys began with Barbie and G.I. Joe dolls, but outside of such old standards as these, most are linked to cartoon series for a very good reason—the series themselves provide half- or full-hour promotions for these products. They don't need paid advertising and they don't buy it. Indeed, when new cartoon series are developed, series toys are developed along with them.

The reduction in toy commercials by 20 minutes from 1990 to 1992 thus pales in comparison with the nearly 8 hours of commercials cartoon programming itself represents. We know that children have a hard time separating fantasy and reality. Young children in particular tend to believe everything they see on television and do not really understand the nature of commercials or commercialism (Beasich et al., 1992; Christenson & Roberts, 1983; Dorr, 1986). The lack of clear delineation between advertising and entertainment can only confuse them more.

Such confusion, of course, mirrors a similar confusion in the larger "shop 'til you drop" culture in which we live, and is obviously not a confusion the advertisers who pay for Saturday morning programming are likely to want to remedy. It may not even be a confusion our advanced capitalist culture itself wants to clear up. After all, a capitalist economy needs an ever increasing demand. What better way to insure such demand than to raise new generations of avid consumers?

DISCUSSION

Saturday morning is the only block of television time devoted exclusively to children. Saturday morning programming is therefore a primary text for children's social learning from television. What does that text teach them about the larger society and how they should behave in it?

It teaches them that White men are the most important and powerful people in that society, that women are underrepresented everywhere, that minorities are excluded in some places, that old people are incompetent and evil and best left alone. It teaches them that the world is a scary place and that its cities are the most scary of all. It teaches them to be active consumers. It teaches them that they should get a good education and show concern for the environment, that they should be courageous, kind, and persistent; but most of all it teaches them that they should belong and be loyal to a group, that they should always cooperate with group members, and that they should never act on their own.

The messages of Saturday morning, therefore, are not really very different from the messages of American society. But are they really the messages we want our children to hear? And if we aren't happy with these messages, is there really much we can do about it? The work of Action for Children's Television (Kaye, 1979) may be instructive in this regard.

Action for Children's Television worked long and hard to change the messages of Saturday morning programming. In some ways it was successful; in some ways it wasn't. Its lobbying efforts, for example, were successful in securing passage of the Children's Television Act of 1990, and so limiting advertising in Saturday morning programming to 2 minutes per hour. Its pressure on advertisers and networks to reduce the violence in cartoons resulted in a thorough reworking of cartoon formulae to produce the derived reality we see on Saturday mornings today. On the other hand, the reduction in advertising time in Saturday morning programming did not really reduce the number of advertising messages it contained, and, even if it had, such reduction would mean little in the context of whole programs that serve to promote products. The derived reality of cartoon stories, although less violent and more cooperative, is arguably scarier, and clearly lacking in both historical and psychological sense.

The work of Action for Children's Television, therefore, tells us that you can change children's programming, but that you don't always get what you really want. In particular, it would be foolish to think that you can change these lesser messages of a society without significantly changing that society itself. It would be foolish to think, for example, that you can change the consumerist messages of Saturday morning programming when that programming is paid for by advertisers in an advanced capitalist culture. It would be foolish to think that the power relationships and fears of American society won't be reflected in the cartoons it produces. It would also probably be foolish to think that stories engineered to meet particular standards won't meet them at the expense of other elements.

So what can be done? One thing that might be done would be to pressure networks and advertisers to produce cartoons based on traditional children's stories. We know that Saturday morning programming can be changed through this sort of pressure, and we know that most cartoons are derived from other sources anyway. I would like to see at least one series based on American history, and another based on classic children's literature. I think a series that dealt with specific values in different episodes would also be a good idea. When my own children were little, we had a series of books called ValueTales (Johnson, 1978) that highlighted specific values through biographies of famous people and which my children really loved. The Children's Television Act of 1990 even provides a legal basis for such pressure in that it requires the holders of television franchises to serve "the educational and informational needs of children through the licensee's overall programming, including programming specifically designed to serve such needs."

In the meantime, as parents and educators we should teach our children to view television critically. We should watch with them and talk to them about the messages in all television programming—Saturday morning programming in particular. In *Amusing Ourselves to Death*, Postman (1986) observed that no matter how bad we think television is, and he thinks it's pretty bad, it isn't going to go away. He argued that we must teach our children about the ways in which television shapes our lives, and the ways in which they can, in turn, shape it to serve our needs. He wrote:

It is an acknowledged task of the schools to assist the young in learning how to interpret the symbols of their culture. That this task should now require that they learn how to distance themselves from their forms of information is not so bizarre an enterprise that we cannot hope for its inclusion in the curriculum, even hope that it will be placed at the center of education. (p. 163)

REFERENCES

Beasich, J., Leinoff, S., & Swan, K. (1992). Saturday morning TV: Kid's perspectives. In K. Swan (Ed.), *Saturday morning: Critical analyses of television cartoon programming* (LTL Report 92-1, pp. 65-93). Albany: SUNY at Albany, Learning Technologies Laboratory.

Bettelheim, B. (1976). *The uses of enchantment: The meaning and importance of fairy tales.* New York: Avon.

Bokan, K. H. (1992). Examination of plots and settings of selected Saturday morning cartoons. In K. Swan (Ed.), *Saturday morning: Critical analyses of television cartoon programming* (LTL Report 92-1, pp. 13-19). Albany: SUNY at Albany, Learning Technologies Laboratory.

Christenson, P. G., & Roberts, D. F. (1983). The role of television in the formation of children's social attitudes. In M.J.A. Howe (Ed.), *Learning from television: Psychological and educational research* (pp. 79-100). New York: Academic Press.

Costanzo, W. V. (1994). Reading Ollie North. In R.F. Fox (Ed.), *Images in language, media, and mind* (pp. 108-122). Urbana, IL: National Council of Teachers of English.

Donelson, K., & Nilsen, A. P. (1989). *Literature for today's young adults* (3rd ed.). Glenview, IL: Scott Foresman.

Dorr, A. (1986). *Television and children: A special medium for a special audience.* Newbury Park, CA: Sage.

Gerbner, G., Gross, L., Morgan, M., & Signorielli, N. (1980). The mainstreaming of America: Violence profile No. 11. *Journal of Communication, 30*(3), 10-29.

Goldberg, M. E., & Gorn, G. J. (1983). Researching the effects of television advertising on children: A methodological critique. In M. A. Howe (Ed.), *Learning from television: Psychological and educational research* (pp. 125-151). London: Academic Press.

Greenless, T., & Swan, K. (1992). Saturday morning commercials and food and beverage advertising for children. In K. Swan (Ed.), *Saturday morning: Critical analyses of television cartoon programming* (LTL Report 92-1, pp. 37-45). Albany: SUNY at Albany, Learning Technologies Laboratory.

Guadagno, P., & Swan, K. (1992). Morality in Saturday morning cartoons. In K. Swan (Ed.), *Saturday morning: Critical analyses of television cartoon programming* (LTL Report 92-1, pp. 2-6). Albany: SUNY at Albany, Learning Technologies Laboratory.

Johnson, S. (1978). *ValueTales*. La Jolla, CA: Value Communications.

Karp, W. (1987). Where the do-gooders went wrong. In H. Newcomb (Ed.), *Television: The critical view* (pp. 433-444). New York: Oxford University Press.

Kaye, E. (1979). *The ACT guide to children's television*. Boston: Beacon Press.

Knowles, J., & Swan, K. (1992). Stereotyping in children's television. In K. Swan (Ed.), *Saturday morning: Critical analyses of television cartoon programming* (LTL Report 92-1, pp. 20-26). Albany: SUNY at Albany, Learning Technologies Laboratory

McCloud, S. (1994). *Understanding comics: The invisible art*. Northampton, MA: Kitchen Sink Publishing.

Meurs, J., & Griffis, N. (1992). Public service announcements shown during Saturday morning cartoons. In K. Swan (Ed.), *Saturday morning: Critical analyses of television cartoon programming* (LTL Report 92-1, pp. 58-63). Albany: SUNY at Albany, Learning Technologies Laboratory.

National Institute of Mental Health. (1982). *Television and behavior: Ten years of scientific progress and implications for the Eighties. Vol. 1: Summary report* (DHHS Publication No. (ADM) 82-1195). Washington DC: U.S. Government Printing Office.

Postman, N. (1986). *Amusing ourselves to death*. New York: Penguin.

6

Broadcast Television: African American Youth Create Their Own Vision

Joseph Bowman
University at Albany

> Many say that the mass media don't want to show anything positive about Blacks because that would compromise the self-esteem of many Whites who base their sense of superior importance on the subjugation of other people.—Nobel (1981, p. 88)

These are hard words to open a discussion about broadcasting and African American youth, but for many people of color these types of statements reflect an area of great concern. For years there has been limited programming about people of color. What existed was generally stereotypical and demeaning. Even now, there are few people of color on news, sitcoms, and evening drama programs.

The hard reality is that television in the United States usually portrays members of minorities as less powerful and poorer than the majority. (Palmer, 1978) This theme is presented on American television daily for minorities and majority children to see and to internalize. This process, occurring in a multiracial society, can cause an identity conflict: How to have the status of a white person, without ceasing to identify psychologically with one's own group? This is an area of real concern to many critics and media scholars. Greenfield (1984), for example, wrote "By constantly presenting an image of Blacks that is negative to their dignity and self-esteem, television helps to perpetuate these identity problems for minority children (p. 43). O'Connor (1991) claimed "Television portrayals of African Americans on television tend to be one dimensional, bordering on buffoons and bumbling idiots" (p. 23). Indeed Williams & Condry (1988), in a review of prime-time programming, found the majority of roles given to actors of color to belong to the lower levels of society.

113

They wrote "While *The Cosby Show* and *The Fresh Prince of Bel Air* show Blacks in professional jobs, most occupations held by Blacks on television tend to be limited to blue-collar fields (p. 47).

Dervin and Greenberg (1972) stated that approximately 95% the of urban poor have at least one television set, and approximately 40% own more than one. Additionally, low–income Blacks watch more television than low-income Whites. Television is gaining ground in high schools because it is the main teenage medium. On average, teenagers spend about 21 hours watching television, as compared with 1.8 hours of reading for pleasure, according to a 1992 report by the Carnegie Council on Adolescent Development. (The Freedom Forum, 1994) According to the cultivation hypothesis, heavier television viewers are more likely to be influenced by the repetitiveness and consistency of portrayals of racial groups (Gerbner, Gross, Morgan, & Signorielli, 1986). Thus, the portrayal of African Americans in the television medium has resulted in a mass of social identity crisis whereby minorities are not only seeing how society defines them, but also how they are being disadvantaged (Meyrowitz, 1985).

Another aspect of the problem facing African American youth is their real-world status. Their socioeconomic status is poor, they live in economically depressed areas, and, most importantly, they are considered "at risk" for academic failure. In New York City, dropout data were broken down by gender and ethnicity. Gender distribution of students from 1987 through 1988 indicated that 56.1% of male high school students and 43.9% of female students dropped out of schools. In *School Dropouts in the United States*, Pallas (1985) gave several reasons why minority students drop out of school. Poor academic performance, student rebelliousness, students working more that 25 hours per week, delinquency or truancy, and teenage pregnancy and/or marriage are all cited. *Black and White Children in America: Key Facts* added the following reasons to the list: language/cultural barriers, lack of supportive relationships, poor home regard and support for education, and burnout from trying too hard to succeed (Children's Defense Fund, 1985).

This chapter discusses a series of programs designed, to address both the media images with which minority youth are bombarded, and the poor academic preparation/aspirations they have for continuing their educations through and beyond high school. In these programs, students use video and other media to produce programs that depict themselves and their community in a positive light. Behind the design of these programs is the belief that positive self-image and positive academic performance go hand in hand. What better way to address both than with the dominant medium of our culture?

THE PROJECTS

In the spring of 1982, the Institute for Urban and Minority Education (IUME) at Teachers College, Columbia University applied for and received a grant to design and implement a telecommunications program for inner-city middle and high school students in the Bronx and Manhattan. These students would not ordinarily be exposed to current applications of new technologies. IUME is concerned with the following questions: How do we begin to bridge the technology gap in this country and, specifically, in the inner city area? How do we provide services and training to the economically disadvantaged who may not otherwise get this opportunity? How do we expose them to the new technologies; that is, video production, computers, teletext, telecommunications, and so on.

In New York City, programs in computers and telecommunications are just beginning to be implemented in a select number of urban city schools. In an interview, the former Executive Director of IUME, the late Dr. Marguerite Ross Barnett-King (personal communication, October 1,1983) summed up the importance of this initiative by saying:

> The Institute is committed to human development at the secondary and high school levels, in all areas of the educational process. Economically disadvantaged students are a major concern and must be provided with the training and guidance to meet the high technology and telecommunications world of the present and the future. The Institute will continue to expand and support projects in these areas and also develop more programs that create opportunities for women. (p. II)

To its credit, IUME has sponsored several technology-based programs over the years, all of which have used television production as their underlying theme. As the technology revolution has evolved to include personal computers, IUME has incorporated that technology into its programs, but television production has been at the core of it all. Bowman (1991) utilized the resources of this work at IUME to complete his dissertation research on designing technology based programs. In 1992, Dr. Bowman and IUME created the Center for Urban Youth and Technology (CUYT) to consolidate its burgeoning technology programs. IUME/CUYT programs have included:

- TeleCommunications Career Development Project (TCCDP) (1982-1985),
- Adolescent Minority Women and the Media Project,(WEEA) (1983-1984),

- Telecommunications and Computer Basic Skills Training Program (1985-1988),
- Technology Education and Career Enhancement Program (TECH).(1990-1994),
- Girl Scout Scholar Program (GSSP) (1990-1993)
- Technology Internship Program (TIP) (1989-Present)
- In-Service Teacher Training Program on Multi-Media Applications (1991-Present)

Each program has been modified to meet the needs and concerns of the audience and present our theme(s) in a uniform and knowledgeable way. These programs have all been based on our concern about minority representation or misrepresentation and/or the representation/misrepresentation of women on broadcast television. The desire was to have students create their own programs that depict themselves and their community in a positive light.

The benefits of developing an African American community whose members are knowledgeable in the use of resources in broadcast television are many and significant. Prime among them is the creation of a network of decision makers in broadcast and other fields (advertising and law) who will be sensitive to the negative effects of stereotypical and demeaning portrayals on television. These programs can also have a neutralizing effect on broadcasting portrayals in several ways. Television can have a positive effect if it portrays minority contributions and involvement in a factual and truthful fashion.

Other benefits include:

- Learning to use television in areas other than television itself, such as in business;
- Learning about team building;
- Building maintaining skills for college and career goals;
- Completing their high school;
- Providing positive role models for their communities and themselves;
- Being instilled with the importance of giving back to their communities to improve the quality of life for the youth that are following them in the near future.

Involvement with the medium can stimulate students to become challenged academically, socially responsible, and technically competent.

The projects set out to create a technology-based program that would use television production techniques to empower middle and high school African American students. They focused on social learning through empowerment, improved self-images, and increased community awareness. In these projects, television was the change agent that stimulated ideas and discussion about how to make television more responsive to the needs and concerns of African American youth. The goal was to develop skills in various aspects of television production while giving them highly developed skills in a specific area of expertise. As Gandy and Matabane (1989) contended, we need more television media presentations created by and for African Americans.

The TeleCommunications Career Development Program (TCCDP) and the Technology Education and Career Enhancement Program (Project TECH) are the primary focus of the discussion that follows. They represent a continuous program design that was only modified by the transition of our program audience from high school to middle school students. This was done to address the growing number of high school students we encountered who felt that they could never complete high school and their concerns about success, self–esteem, and empowerment. The Center for Urban Youth and Technology realized that if African American high school youth are to succeed, they must receive guidance and support in the earlier grades. The two programs became extensions of each other. The Technology Intern Program (TIP) was designed to meet the needs of continuing students. These programs recruited students from Brandeis and John F. Kennedy high schools and middle school students from Roberto Clemente and Adam Clayton Powell Jr. middle schools in the Bronx and upper Manhattan.

THEORETICAL BASIS FOR CURRICULUM DESIGN

Our curriculum design was exploratory and open ended to allow for modifications and input from students and teachers and grounded in Bruner's (1966) notion of *guided discovery learning*. Bruner stated:

> A curriculum reflects not only the nature of the knowledge itself but also the nature of the knower and of the knowledge-getting process. . . . To instruct someone in these disciplines is not a matter of getting him to commit results to mind. Rather, it is to teach him to participate in the process that makes possible the establishment of knowledge. (p. 72)

Teaching through discovery is time consuming, but the benefits include greater long-term recall and better transfer of skills. Moreover, this type of curriculum design allows and encourages participant engagement, involvement, and attitudes critically important to our purposes. Television and computers are fascinating devices that provide the opportunity for hands on activities. We used the medium to teach the medium and provided students with the opportunity to learn in a nonthreatening environment. While students were at "play" and having "fun," they learned how to use the equipment (cameras, microphones, and computers). Teachers provided assistance as it was needed while they monitored activities and group project goals. Team teaching techniques were employed in all classroom activities, using a collaborative constructivist learning model. We trained teachers to work as a team, to have a strong knowledge of their subject areas, to be sensitive to students' needs, and to have a sense of their community.

We also incorporated the notion of Dr. Edwin Nickols (1991) on teaching African American children into the curriculum design. Dr. Nickols looks at philosophical constructs and their cross-cultural implications for learning. In *Cultural Foundations for Teaching Black Children*, he stated:

> The education of Black children in America has been ineffective. . . .
> Many educators fail to recognize important cultural differences
> between Europeans or Euro-Americans and African or African
> Americans. . . . In the schooling process, children from one ethnic
> group are expected to use some of the problem solving strategies of
> other groups. Inevitably, however, serious cross-cultural problems
> arise. (p. 51)

Nickols believes that Black children learn best from "peer learning," where they are paired together during instruction. Placing black students in small groups in an open classroom therefore facilitates learning.

This conceptual framework provided important elements in preparing instructors for teaching with this student population. It gave our instructors another paradigm to use in developing curriculum and program concepts. Nickols' concepts required instructors and administrators in the program to evaluate their own teaching methods and identify ways that their instruction could be enhanced. Instructors consequently looked at the culture of the students they would be teaching. Indeed these concerns and ideas resonate throughout the programs that were developed.

TEACHER TRAINING

Because of logistical and resource constraints, curriculum development centered on the television resources of Teachers College, Columbia University. When developing a technology-based program, an instructional design delineating the integration of technology with regular coursework is critical. Students, instructors, parents, and administrators must understand how the curriculum will evolve and how it will be integrated with instruction in basic skills areas. Important considerations must be given to the standardized examinations, which are a mandatory part of the New York City school environment. Many administrators and teachers insist on using technology to bring standardized exam scores higher at their school. Our approach, however, was to provide the technology as a tool to enhance the curriculum and not focus specifically on this one aspect of its potential. We decided that teachers would be the best arbitrators of curriculum integration. Thus teacher training was a very important component of our programs. It was held before the programs started and minisessions continued throughout the program cycle. The training provided an introduction to video production, computer skills, suggestions for curriculum integration, including examples showing how they could use television and computer technology in their classroom activities. Teachers were then given time to review existing curriculum to determine how they would incorporate the technology into their classroom activities and lesson plans. Minisessions held throughout the program cycle were used to review and revise integration activities and to provide ongoing support for innovation. Teachers worked on individual programs, included video literacy, research, word processing, script writing, story boarding, production, and editing components. These are explained in the sections that follow.

Video Literacy

Our vision was to build a general television production curriculum that could be used by middle and high school students in relation to a variety of specific curriculum goals. Within these general guidelines, students were to create their own programs that demonstrated the positive attitudes and contributions of people of African American descent. These programs would be viewed on public-access cable television and shared with other youth around the city, state, and country. Our goal was to help students portray their communities, culture, and situation from their own perspective and to share that experience with others. We began by sensitizing them to video programming.

We asked students to review existing programming on broadcast television and to discuss their findings in terms of what television is suggesting about their social conditions. For video literacy development, students were asked to monitor what they viewed for 2 weeks and report the findings to the class for presentation and discussion. Students were provided with guidelines to evaluate the programs they watched, but not given required programs or time slots. This process continued informally throughout the programs. For example, students were asked to watch television programs as a director and list the camera shot selections that were used during that program to see how shot selection affected the quality and presentation of a program and learn the language of broadcast television production. They were asked to provide an overview of a program's theme, characters, and plot development. As a whole class, students were also asked to watch television with the sound off to see if they could identify visual cues. Students then turned the sound on and darkened the picture to see if the audio track kept them involved in the program. Students were asked to comment on both processes. Whenever possible, we asked students to include family members in similar activities to get their ideas, viewing patterns, and concerns about television. Samples of old viewing patterns, production treatments, production shots sheets, and program scripts were also provided and discussed.

Research

Video literacy activities also prompted students to think about various themes and television productions that they might produce. Before they could begin production, however, they were required to do several things. The first was to research their topic. They were introduced to a variety of research techniques including library research, interviewing techniques, gathering information from their communities, and electronic researching via the Internet. They were then asked to use these skills to develop a treatment of a program that they would produce. A treatment is a description of the production that will be produced and includes program format, staff selection, explanation of program content, site location, budget, and story board. Students were also required to present their treatments to the whole class for review and comment.

Word Processing

While amassing and organizing material for their video literacy and research assignments, students learned to use word processing. They word processed a journal of television notes that focused on programs they watched and included findings and discussions which evolved in class. Research notes and program treatments were also developed with word processors, as were the productions scripts. All of these activities were designed to develop students writing and work processing skills within a meaningful context. There were also intended to show them the advantages of computing skills. These skills were extended to the use of graphic programs when preproductions activities turned to storyboarding. They were all stored on the computer and on individual student computer disks.

Script Writing

Once treatments were reviewed and revised, students turned them into scripts, which were created using the word processor. A script had to be prepared for each production treatment that students developed. A series of script-writing exercises were presented to the students during the class to introduce them to writing for television. They were also reminded about the importance of presenting positive images of African American roles in their script development.

Storyboarding

Storyboarding provides a representation of the visual and audio aspects of a television program before the program goes into the production phase. After their scripts were developed, students were asked to visualize what the television program (commercial, public service announcement, or television program) would look like. They were then taught storyboarding techniques, which required them to place the script (audio), duration of the segment (time), and a visual representation (screen) of each shot in a standardized format, so that all elements of the production can be reviewed for concepts, potential problems, and problem solutions. Students used the cut-and-paste features of the computer to combine text (scripts) and graphics (screens) to create storyboards of their productions.

Video Productions

This is a small sample of production projects in which students have been involved and provides a perspective of production activities that our programs supported. Commercials and public service announcements (PSAs) were the first productions that all students were required to produce and they proved to be very exciting and unique. Topics included standard product commercials where students made up the names to PSAs about drug use, teen pregnancy, violence, and teen suicide. All of these PSAs and commercials were screened and selected for segues between segments of the news programs that the students produced.

The students also produced news programs that had complete minority representation in their on-air personnel. They determined what topics were important and then researched the material for that segment. The news programs used similar news program formats (local, national, sports, and weather) but were presented from the perspective of the students and their viewing audience.

Another type of program created was the variety show. The variety show format presented African American and Hispanic people the students felt represented positive role images for their audience. The students would create short vignettes to provide the viewer with a sense of the character of each person and a skit to dramatize a specific point in that person's life.

Finally, some students created whole documentary programs. Subjects were determined by the concerns of the students who volunteered to work with the Youth Lobby Day activities. Their work involved documenting pre-lobby-day events in New York City where young lobbyists learned how to lobby and select a assembly person or senator to lobby. The students then traveled to Albany, NY to meet elected officials, Assembly persons, and Senators. As a result of this work, the students were asked to document the public hearings on "Violence as a Public Health Issue" for Brooklyn cable television and the office of Assemblyman Roger Green.

In 1990, our students were asked to cover Nelson Mandela's trip to New York City and received State Department Press Credentials to attend all press activities. The students set up location assignments for the 4 days of events and activities all around the New York City area (Yankee Stadium, Brooklyn Academy of Music, United Nations, Harlem outdoor rally, Riverside Church). After the event, they expressed concern that they were the only youth production team to get the proper press credentials for this international event.

The International Youth Leadership Institute (IYLI) sponsors trips to foreign countries for youth every year and requested that a youth production crew to travel overseas to document the experience. Students from TCCDP were assigned the task of setting up this production and planning travel to Egypt. They had created interviews, questions, developed a script, decided what equipment should be taken on the trip, obtained the correct travel documents (visa and press credentials), determined how to charge batteries with foreign current (power) standards, and learned the language of the country.

Video Editing

The final phase of video production involves editing footage into a complete program. Students learned how to use the editors by creating small shows using existing footage from other productions. This practice prepared them to work on their own productions. They also discussed the importance of creating a good video production plan, getting quality video, and creating a team that could then edit it into an excellent program. If all elements of the production came together, the postproduction editing would go smoothly because all problems had been discussed and resolved beforehand.

OUTCOMES

The processes involved in the video production programs we designed, focused on developing the personal and social identities as well as the academic and video production skills of the students involved. They differed from other instructional experiences in several ways. First, the format provided students with an environment in which instructional experiences were open, supportive, and challenging. Second, they were student-centered: Productions were the creations of the students. Third, programs were designed to develop students' skills in a meaningful context, concerned with their own life experiences. We believe this concern for students' lives is a critical element in our programs. Other research supports this observation: "Efforts must extend to the multiple settings within which the child lives (for example, the home, the school, the peer group), that is, the areas of the community within which the child interacts when not in school" (Dryfoos, 1990, p. 128).

Because of this particular orientation to students' lives, we expected students outcomes to include social learning and empowerment, and literacy. Social learning is linked to the development of a community of learners who are sensitive both to the needs of that community and the impact that broadcast television has on them. Empowerment relates to how students feel about themselves and see themselves in society. This is reinforced through the roles they play in their communities. Literacy refers to the development of video literacy, basic academic skills and television production expertise. Each of these are explored, in turn, in the sections that follow. Finally the most important outcome, the students' productions themselves are briefly reviewed.

Social Learning

In the area of social learning, the project fostered a community of learners sensitive to the needs of their communities and concerned about the impact that broadcast television has on them. Support for this result can be found in the television program concepts that they generated and their involvement in community activities. Initially, students produced commercials (for sneakers, hair spray, candy), but sometime during the year we noticed a shift from these to PSAs on community-based and youth-oriented themes. We believe this reflected a shift in what was important to them. In addition, some of the students joined community organizations that worked with youth to support their initiatives, learn new things, and to keep themselves off the streets. All became more aware of activities that would lead to social and personal development, and training for college and careers. Processes used to evaluate social learning included observations of group sessions, direct involvement in group discussions, monitoring video production concepts, and student involvement in outside program activities.

Empowerment

Empowerment refers to the development of positive image perceptions and self-esteem. Our counselors play a critical role in this regard. When the program was originally developed, the need for counseling seemed small. We discovered very quickly that all of our students carried personal and social baggage into the program with them. The baggage stemmed from home life, school life, and street survival, and played itself out several times during the program. With counselors integrated into the classroom activities, we were able to identify problems and intervene when necessary. Many problems were concerned with self-identity and low self-esteem issues. Most were related to the "at-risk" label. "At risk" to these students meant inferiority, stupidity and, Black and/or minority status. Many of the students in the program had heard this term used to refer to them for several years in elementary and middle school. Coupled with racial stigmas, low self-esteem, and the negative images of minorities portrayed on television, this labeling is what the students related as the cause of their academic and social frustrations.

One goal was to let the students know that their frustrations were warranted and that they could use the skills they were acquiring (television and desktop publishing) to express themselves. Because the program was project-oriented and included numerous small tasks on the way to video production, students began to feel accomplished. If support was needed, student teams were formed so that they could work together to solve their problems. Individualized support was given when students requested assistance. Accomplishments were acknowledged, awards were given, and praise communicated to students' parents. Many students were even asked to serve as program spokespersons at conferences, presentations, and television interviews.

As students' self-esteem and self-worth began to increase, their involvement in the program's activities began to change. Students that were passive and subdued joined teams and became integral players in the productions. Some became spokespersons at events. Many would discuss their ideas and present solutions to television production problems to other students and parents interested in these issues. Student grades began to increase in school as they transferred their feelings of competency within the program to their traditional classroom experiences.

Literacy

Literacy refers to video literacy skills, basic academic skills (writing, math, and reading), and video production skills. Assessment of literacy outcomes involved a combination of task-related presentations, pre- and post-testing in specific subject areas, and portfolio assessment.

The students applied video literacy skills while watching television at home. The television program viewing list that they created was discussed in class and then combined with those of other students to form a viewing chart. This chart would be modified during the school year but provided a overview of what students were watching. This was important when we asked them to watch a specific program and comment on the character roles, shot selection, and program content. The students were asked to be television directors and identify camera shots in television programs. This technique reinforced the terms and television language that they would use in later productions. Outcomes for completion of video literacy skills were assessed through a review of students' viewing pattern journals, shot selection logs, use of television language and terms, and classroom discussions about television.

In terms of video productions skills, a checklist on using equipment was given to students. They were responsible for deciding which items they were ready to complete. Working with the instructor, they demonstrated the specific requirements associated with each piece of equipment. At the end of 3 months, students were to have completed 80% of the checklist. This technique was used to help them stay abreast of what areas they needed to learn. All of the students in the programs completed the checklist. Students also demonstrated their technical skills by the quality of their productions. They quickly learned that production skills and equipment operation were critical elements in the success and completion of television productions.

Basic skills (reading, writing, and math) were always a primary focus of our programs, but we could not focus on them directly for fear of alienating students frustrated by their "at-risk" labeling. Instead, basic skills were incorporated into program development activities where students were led to appreciate and discover the importance of skills development on their own. When the students were producing these television productions, two aspects of the processes emerged. They had to create scripts for the production and they had to read scripts before the television camera. Because there was always a time limit for the scripts and narration on camera, math skills were also brought into play. Basic English and math skills became important without our saying a word. Students started looking for dictionaries, asking about usage and tense in sentence structure, and looking for a stop watch to time how long each script took. Writing became very important. Students started using electronic dictionaries, typing tutors, and English language software. Student journals, scripts, and program treatments were all completed using the computer.

Gains on standardized tests indicated our programs were extremely successful. Tenth- and 11th-grade students improved their scores by one grade level in reading and math. The high school students showed an improvement of two grade levels in both subject areas. Several students also took the New York State Regents' Competency Tests (RCT). Seventy-five percent of them passed in all three areas (reading, math, and writing).

Teachers at participating schools were also asked a range of questions to determine if they saw any changes in students' attitudes and behavior. Survey results indicate that 50% of the students showed increased interest in asking questions and volunteering to answer questions in class. The results also showed that 56% to 60% showed improvement in the organization and the quality of their writing. Teachers indicated that 28% of students stated opinions and beliefs, and 25% showed good insight, creativity, and originality. Dr. Dalton Miller-Jones (1987), an external evaluator, suggested that these changes may have been the result of students talking before the video camera, acting out roles in the commercials they produced, and the critiquing they did of their own and others' performances.

Productions

Perhaps the most positive outcome of our programs were the students productions themselves. Students responded to the need for relevant programming about African Americans on broadcast television by producing programs that showed minorities as central characters in positive roles. They developed programs that had a sense of community and which related to their communities' goals. Program formats were chiefly news, documentary, variety programs with commercials, and PSAs. The latter treated topics such as violence, gangs, drugs, teen pregnancy, empowerment, suicide, and cultural awareness.

News programs had complete minority representation in their on air talent. All newscasters were African American and Hispanic, reflecting the population that students felt should be served by their programming. The news programs used common news program formats (local, national, sports, and weather) but were presented from the perspective of the students and their viewing audience. Students determined what topics were important and then researched that material.

Variety shows presented African American and Hispanic people that students felt presented positive role models. The students developed short vignettes of individual personalities to provide viewers with a sense of their characters. They then created a skit to dramatize a specific important point in time of that person's life. The purpose was to show strong family life in the African American and Hispanic community and to counteract the negative images of African Americans and Hispanics on broadcast television.

The students felt that they were making a difference because of the programs they produced. Cable television viewers responded by sending correspondence about the programs. Many students asked about joining the program after seeing a broadcast on cable television. This impressed on our students the fact that they too could demonstrate how they viewed relevant programming about African Americans and Hispanics. They, in turn, wrote letters to program producers and expressed their views about the content of broadcast television programs.

DISCUSSION

In a recent study, Winborne, Nesbitt and Ballard (1995), looked at self-image, adult image, and child image of preschoolers. The study indicated that African American and European American preschoolers were nearly equal in their perceptions of self and appeared to maintain equally positive views of children within their respective racial groups. In regard to adult images, European American children maintained positive views about children and adults within their racial group. African American children were less positive in their perceptions of adult African Americans. African American male adults were viewed more negative by both groups. Negative responses were nearly always made when African American male images were presented. Why is this happening? The study's authors contend that "While positive race and self images are generally maintained by and about African Americans during childhood, these views might be negatively influenced by societal values and media portrayals over time" (Winborne, Nesbitt, & Ballard, 1995, pp. 1-6)

The impact of negative role images on broadcast television begins in the early viewing years (Saturday morning and weekday children's programming) and continues during a child's elementary, middle, and high school years. It has the potential to scar the self-image, and a community's sense of self-worth.

Involvement in television production can turn this trend around by creating a community of learners who can produce programs that show positive images of minorities. Students participating in this project have raised their self-esteem and motivation through their accomplishments. They have made contributions to their community by serving as peer counselors, peer tutors, peer instructors, and spokespersons on issues relating to youth and the community. Many of these learners came to take education seriously, graduated from high school, and went on to college. Several have entered the broadcast industry to perfect their craft. They are beginning to make changes from within the system. Others have decided to look at other professions (advertising and corporate business-es that support programs) which relate to broadcast television and see how they can impact programming. A few have decided to create their own production companies to produce socially relevant programs. In all cases, our students are positively contributing to society.

REFERENCES

Bowman, J., Jr. (1991). Documenting a technology-based telecommunica-tions program for urban youth: Its impact and future role in high school retention. *Dissertation Abstracts International, 52,* 7.

Bruner, J.S. (1966) *Toward a theory of instruction.* New York: Norton.

Children's Defense Fund. (1985). *Black and White children in America: Key facts.* Washington, DC: Author.

Dervin, B., & Greenberg, B.S. (1972). The communications environment of the urban poor. In F.G. Kline & P. Tichenor (Eds.), *Current per-spectives in mass communication research* (pp. 195-233). Newbury Park, CA: Sage.

Dryfoos, J. G. (1990). *Adolescents at risk: Prevalence and prevention.* New York: Oxford University Press.

The Freedom Forum. (1994). *Death by cheeseburger: High school journalism in the 1990s and beyond.* New York: Freedom Forum.

Gandy, I. H., & Matabane, P. W. (1989). Television and social perceptions among African Americans and Hispanics. In M. K. Asante & W. B. Gudykunst (Eds.), *Handbook of international and intercultural communi-cations* (pp. 318–348) Newbury Park: Sage.

Gerbner, G., Gross, L. M., Morgan, M., & Signorielli, N. (1986). Living with television: The dynamics of the cultivation process. In J. Bryant & D. Zillman (Eds.), *Perspectives in media effects* (pp. 17-40). Hillsdale, NJ: Erlbaum.

Greenfield, P. M. (1984). *Mind and media: The effects of television, video games and mind.* Cambridge, MA: Harvard University Press.

Meyrowitz, J. (1985). *No sense of place: The impact of electronic media on social behavior.* New York: Oxford University Press.

Miller-Jones, D. (1987), *Telecommunication, computers, and basic skills pro-gram evaluation report.* New York: City of New York Graduate School, Department of Developmental Psychology.

Nickols E., (1991). Cultural foundations of teaching Black children. In *Teaching mathematics* (pp. 51–56). Washington DC: Institute for Independent Education.

Nobel, G. (1981). *Black is the color of my TV tube.* New York: Lyle Stuart.

O'Connor, J. J. (1991, October 28). Black images on TV: Do they really reflect the African-American community? *The Times Herald Record,* pp. 23–29.

Pallas, A. (1985). *School dropouts in the United States, an issue paper.* Washington DC: US Government Printing Office.

Palmer, E. L. (1978). *A pedagogical analysis of recurrent formats on Sesame Street and* The Electronic Company. Paper presented at the International Conference on Children's Educational Television, Amsterdam, and the Annual Conference Convention of the National Association of Educational Broadcasters, Washington, DC.

Williams, M., & Condry, J. C. (1988). *Living color: Minority portrayals and cross-racial interactions in television.* Unpublished manuscript, Cornell University, New York.

Winborne, D.G., Nesbitt, M., & Ballard, S., (1995, April). *Prime reflections: Explorations of racial perceptions among African American and European American preschoolers.* Poster presentation at the American Educational Research Association Conference, San Francisco, CA.

Author Index

Subject Index